™

HAMPTON COURT:
Growing Up Catholic in Indianapolis Between the Wars

by

LAWRENCE S. CONNOR

Guild Press of Indiana
Indianapolis, IN 46208

Guild Press of Indiana, Inc.
6000 Sunset Lane
Indianapolis, IN 46208
Tel.: 317-253-0097
FAX 317-465-1884

Library of Congress Catalog Card Number
95-75392

ISBN: 1-878208-56-X

CONTENTS

INTRODUCTION

This book began as an attempt to capture for my children something of what their paternal grandparents were like and what it was like growing up in Indianapolis between two world wars.

But as I researched the subject and called on what was left of a fading memory I thought others might identify with the time and place where we grew up. That would be Hampton Court, a large apartment complex a block north of the old Cathedral High School, a mile and half north of downtown Indianapolis on North Meridian Street. The site now is occupied by a motel.

The lives we led there in the Thirities were typical of those experienced by thousands of other children, especially those educated and governed by the Catholic Church.

While I have concentrated on telling the story of my own family, I believe others will see something of themselves in the various members. I have also tried to recreate something of what Indianapolis was like in those days.

The Depression that ruled our lives in the 1930s tried the souls of most of the adults but in an odd way it strengthened them, as well. For the children in Hampton Court, though, it was a time of joy and innocence, an innocence erased forever by a second world war.

I have included in the book parts of two articles I had written previously; one for *The Indianapolis Star Magazine* about the SS. Peter & Paul Cathedral (June 25, 1978), and the other a memoir about the 1943 Class at Cathedral High School included in the recently-published book, *Cathedral, Seventy-Five Years*, by Bill Shover and James Obergfell.

I am indebted to many persons for allowing me to tap into their memories. They include my sisters, Sally Lynch and Virginia Grande; sisters-in-law, Toni Scheller Connor and Mary Harrison Connor; cousins Joan Muller, Vincentia Martin, Rita Hennessy, Jim and Jack Connor, and my niece Tina Connor. I also wish to thank Theresa Kast and Robert French for their comments about rooming with us in Hampton Court; Jean Osborne Gill for sharing some of her memories of growing up in the court; Congressman Andy Jacobs for supplying reports from the *Congressional Record* on the recount of an election that bumped an uncle from Congress; Sister Ann Kathleen Brawley, Director of Archives at St. Mary-of-the-Woods, for her assistance in gathering information about my maternal grandparents; George Sippell and Howard Caldwell for their aid; researchers at the Indianapolis-Marion County Public Library and the Indiana State Library, and the General Services Administration at the Minton Capehart Federal Building. And I am especially grateful to Richard E. Cady for his suggestions on the organization of the book, and to Nancy Niblack Baxter for her editing and advice.

Photo credits include former *Star* photographers George A. Newhouse, Frank H. Fisse, Herb Rhodes, and the late William A. Oates, and the late Robert Lavelle of *The Indianapolis News*.

Resources included *The Indianapolis Star* and *The Indianapolis News; Indianapolis, The Story of a City* by Edward A. Leary; *Indiana Through Tradition and Change 1920-1945* (Volume V of the History of Indiana) by James H. Madison; *Hoosier City, The Story of Indianapolis* by Jeannette Covert Nolan; *My Indiana* by Irving Leibowitz; *Indiana Authors and Their Books* by R. E. Banta; *Indianapolis: Hoosiers' Circle City* by George W. Geib; *Indiana: An Interpretation* by John Bartlow Martin; *Biographic History of Eminent & Self-made Men of State of Indiana*, Vol. 1, 1880; *The History of the Catholic Church in Indiana*, Volume 2, published 1898.

*This book is dedicated to my wife, Patty,
and our six children, Carrie, Julie, Larry, Maureen,
Janet and Michael*

A Selfless Woman

My mother, Agnes Peelle Connor, who reared six children with love, discipline and an endless supply of aphorisms, was a rarity in twentieth century America—a dedicated Catholic who truly followed the dictum of carrying out God's work here on earth.

If there was a need that she could fulfill, she filled it. She never gave the impression that she had any needs and wants of her own. If someone was sick or troubled, she was there. If a friend died, she was at the wake. If someone did anything of consequence, she was quick to mail off a note of congratulations.

At our home in Hampton Court, the largely Catholic apartment complex near the old Cathedral High School, she was completely selfless. Long after the rest of us had gone upstairs to read or sleep, Mother was in the basement washing or ironing, then upstairs to set the breakfast table, squeezing oranges or preparing grapefruits, straightening up the living room, and mending clothes. She rarely got to bed before midnight and she was the first one up in the morning. After she got everyone off to school or work she headed for the Cathedral for daily communion.

Theresa Kast, who roomed with us when we lived in Hampton Court in the thirties, still recalls her a half century later as the "most Christian person I've known."

When we were growing up, though, we took Mom for granted. She ran the house, corrected and guided her children, nursed them when they became ill, supported them when they were troubled. She gave. We took—and usually without thanks.

Mother had an aphorism for any occasion. Aphorisms rolled out of her.

If we did a sloppy job, she reminded us that "Anything worth doing is worth doing well."

"If you can't say something nice about someone don't say anything at all," she would interject if she heard us gossiping. When the talk got raunchy, she would retort, "I wouldn't hold in my hand what just came out of your mouth."

1

There was a steady outpouring of advice cloaked in those ancient bromides: don't look a gift horse in the mouth...don't air your dirty linen in public...money doesn't grow on trees...don't judge a book by its cover...your eyes are bigger than your stomach...beggars can't be choosers...if the shoe fits wear it...the road to hell is paved with good intentions.

On and on they rolled out of her.

She was big on advice, too: "Don't slouch...stand up straight...you'll ruin your eyes reading in that light...don't talk with your mouth full...smoking will stunt your growth...don't interrupt...hold your horses...you've got a boarding house reach."

If things weren't going well, she'd suggest that we "offer it up for the poor souls in Purgatory."

Mother never questioned the Church, its teachings or its Pope, though she was known to comment about an exasperating nun, "Just because they put a habit on her doesn't make her a saint."

She was faithful about daily communion, regular confession, and Benediction at four o'clock on Sundays. When there was a novena or a Forty Hours devotion at church, she was there.

Yet she never came across as holy or pious. She was full of life with a great sense of humor, often sprinkling her speech with "damns" and "hells" when she was angry or irritated. But off-color jokes offended her.

Everyone called her Ag, in time even her own children. She was one of those women who made friends easily and kept them for life.

A woman of tremendous energy, she seemed to race through life, striding along, her head pitched forward on her short stout body. She never showed much style when we were growing up, wearing her long gray hair twirled into a bun at the back of her head. She had a pleasant face because it was quick to smile, but she didn't use cosmetics, certainly not lipstick. She was always tightly trussed with a corset, and her dresses were mostly nondescript cotton. In her later years her daughters and daughters-in-law induced her to visit the beauty shop to get her hair permed and set, and made sure that she bought somewhat fashionable clothes, though she didn't give much thought to such adornments.

Consumed by an endless series of tasks, her days were full: scrubbing the week's laundry on a washboard in the basement each Monday, and ironing the clothes on Tuesday. Most of the furnaces in the neighborhood were coal-burning and the soot generated showed up on window sills each morning, forcing her to mop and dust and vacuum almost daily. Mother baked pies and cakes and cookies, using a large cutting board and a rolling pin, but cooking as such never interested her. She, like most women in those days, scrubbed floors on her knees; patched clothes and darned socks, and at least once a year hauled out the rugs and draped them over the clothesline where she beat the dirt out of them with brooms.

She raced from the drug store to the cleaners to the bank, usually winding up at the Piggly Wiggly behind the Court to buy the day's groceries. She was up and down so often at meals that she was always eating cold food after the last of us had left the table.

Mother was no pushover for her children. She didn't hesitate to discipline us when we got out of line. Foul or vulgar language brought out a bar of soap that she made us bite into. Strangely, girls never seemed to utter vulgarities; it wasn't ladylike.

She was attractive as a young woman. She and Dad met in 1911 and were married on a Wednesday morning, June 5, 1912, in St. Joseph's Church by the pastor, Rev. F. B. Dowd. They were both twenty-five years old. Her brother Bob gave her away and Dad's best man was her other brother Maurie. Dad's sister Florence was bridesmaid and his brother Art and a friend, Francis Jordan, were ushers.

The newspaper account reported of the couple:

"Mr. Connor is a well known young man, a prominent K. of C. and his bride is one of the city's best known and most popular young ladies."

The account also stated that "A limousine whisked the bridal party to the future home of the couple immediately after the wedding Mass." That home was at 2347 North Delaware Street.

They had a brief honeymoon at Lake Wawasee. It was there that Mother said she told Dad, "Nick, you've got to start thinking of 'we' rather than 'I' now that we're married." He tried to comply. After an afternoon walk along a dusty lakeside path, Dad suggested, "Let's go in and change our pants."

If we turned up ill, her first question was always, "Did you have a bowel movement this morning?" If we didn't, out came the castor oil in a glass of orange juice.

She treated chest colds by ordering us to bed and smearing warm Vic's VapoRub on our chests and covering it with a warm woolen rag.

She attacked stiff necks by rubbing the area around the collar bone and ending up by twisting our head back and forth, finally snapping it into place—a practice she learned from Dr. C. B. Blakeslee, the osteopath who delivered some of her babies at the Clark-Blakeslee Osteopathic Hospital at 1116 North Delaware Street. She was a great believer in osteopathy.

She liked having one of us reciprocate and give her shoulder and neck "treatments" or scratch her back.

She told me that she employed a different remedy when I was suffering from a severe earache as a nine-month-old baby. Nothing seemed to stop my screaming until she said a prayer and placed a medal of a saint (St. Jude?) against my ear. She said I stopped crying immediately. I was taken to the hospital where I underwent a mastoidectomy.

When Dad was alive, Mother confined her social activities pretty much to watching her sons perform in football and basketball games, though she was in the school Mother's Club and the Altar Society at SS. Peter & Paul Cathedral. She enjoyed attending the meetings of the Procter Club, the Catholic literary club that her mother had helped found in 1898.

After Dad died she helped to establish a local Catholic Interacial Council, and the Guardian Angel Guild for the St. Mary Child Center. She spent hundreds of evenings calling on troubled souls as a member of the Legion of Mary.

One of the highlights of Mother's life were the years she served on the Indianapolis Board of Park Commissioners. Dad had been dead eight years when the newly-elected mayor, Al G. Feeney, appointed her to the board in January, 1948. She was elected president at her initial meeting. She served on the board under four other mayors until 1959. She also served on the boards of two other agencies: the City Plan Commission and the Board of Zoning Appeals. None of the posts paid but no matter; she loved the people and the work in City Hall.

Though an outspoken Democrat, she had very little understanding of ward politics.

"She liked being on all those boards because it got her out of the house," my sister Sally explained. "If she'd had a car we'd never have seen her. She loved to be going somewhere."

Mother, like Dad, never learned to drive because we never owned a car, but she always found a ride.

In time she was recognized for her work, receiving the St. John Bosco medal for her service to the Catholic Youth Organization, and the Pro Ecclesia et Pontifice award from Pope Pius XII.

During the war she and our Aunt Mary Connor, who also lived in Hampton Court with her husband and eight children, helped to set up centers for servicemen at the Knights of Columbus hall at 13th and Delaware streets and at St. John's Catholic Church. Few Sundays went by that Mother didn't bring home for dinner one or more of the young servicemen she had met at the centers. She helped arrange weddings for two young women in service stationed in the city.

Many nights after everyone had gone to bed, Mother would be at her desk scribbling off notes and letters to boys and girls in service, or to their parents, to priests, friends, acquaintances who had done some noteworthy work, and even Hollywood actors and actresses (all Catholic, of course) commending them for some performance or some activity they had carried out. She wrote so swiftly that her sentences ran uphill. Every now and then one of her commendations showed up in the newspaper as a letter to the editor. Occasionally she would send off to *Readers Digest* and the *Catholic Digest* brief anecdotes the magazines sometimes used as fillers.

Mother was gregarious and writing letters was one way to fulfill the need to communicate with others. She got very little conversation from Dad. He spent the evening listening to the radio, reading the newspaper and heading for bed by ten o'clock.

She had always liked writing, beginning as a newspaper reporter in the years before her marriage. She was assistant society editor of *The Indianapolis Star* and later worked for the *Indianapolis Sun*, forerunner of the old *Indianapolis Times*.

She enjoyed talking about those years on the papers. One story she told concerned one of the city's bluebloods, Sylvester Johnson, a world traveler. Johnson believed that he had something to say about any area in the world that happened to be in the news, so he often showed up in the newspaper office, always insisting, of course, that he didn't want publicity.

One morning Mother said she was in the office reading a story about some foreign uprising and remarked: "It's about time for Sylvester to show up." She looked up and he was standing in the doorway looking at her.

Mother had memorized the name of a woman she had come across frequently from her days at *The Star*. We loved having her rattle off the name for our friends and she always obliged. It sounded like this:

"Blanche Maude Mary Capitola Leona Perdida Anna Lena Gentleista Veronica Bloor Schleppy."

She quit her job after marriage. Running a house and raising six children had also forced Mom to give up being active in church or community activities. She had been active in school affairs at St. Mary Academy, where she was the sole graduate in her class; mainly because the other girls enrolled in two-year, rather than four-year, courses of study.

She was a joiner as a young woman. An item in a 1908 newspaper mentioned that she was the president of the Novice Club at St. Joseph's Church. The club raised funds for relief.

Mother didn't get her Catholicity from her father, William A. Peelle, a Presbyterian. He died of a heart attack at the age of forty-nine in 1894 when Mother was just seven years old. His death came just three days after the family had arrived at St. Mary-of-the-Woods in Terre Haute where the parents had gone to jointly manage the new Woodland Inn on the campus. Her strong Catholic faith was a legacy of her mother, Margaret FitzGibbon Peelle.

Unlike Mother, Dad had little interest in the church. He gave it one hour each Sunday morning, attending Mass (but never receiving communion) to set an example for his children. It gave him an opportunity to buy a *Chicago Tribune* from the newshawk outside the Cathedral.

Mother grew up within a half mile of the home of James Whitcomb Riley, the Hoosier poet. She loved his homey poems, often

A Political Family

Both of Mother's parents were active in Indiana politics. Her mother, Margaret FitzGibbon Peelle, was elected state librarian in 1879. That year she married William A. Peelle, the deputy secretary of state, a post he held until he was elected state statistician three years later. Both were Democrats.

They had met in the old Indiana Statehouse and were married when both were in their mid-thirties. In the next eight years they had five children, one of whom died at the age of nine months.

Margaret Peelle was something of a nineteenth century feminist, using her political clout as a friend of four Indiana governors to lobby for the appointment of women to state boards at a time when few women were active in politics.

She was one of fourteen children, seven of whom died in infancy. Her parents had immigrated from County Cork in 1821 to escape persecution by the British. Two of her father's brothers had been sentenced to die with the famed Irish patriot, Robert Emmet, following the unsuccessful rebellion he led in 1803. The brothers later got reprieves and were exiled for life to the island of Martinique. One of them escaped to the United States, the other died in exile.

Ironically, my Grandfather Peelle was of British stock, a member of a prominent Eastern Indiana family of Republicans. His brother, Stanton J. Peelle, served a term in Congress until he was ousted by a questionable recount and later became chief justice of the United States Court of Claims in Washington, D. C.

reciting his verses to us: "Little Orphant Annie's come to our house to stay, an' wash the cups an' saucers up, an' brush the crumbs away..." When Fall came she would recite, "When the frost is on the punkin and the fodder's in the shock..."

Mother contended that she was Riley's second cousin, but she didn't brag about it, perhaps because Riley had a reputation of being a boozer, and he was not Catholic, in her view an undesirable combination.

Mother had been told by her parents that she was a distant relative of Sir Robert Peel, who is considered Britain's greatest prime minister, serving in 1834-35 and again in 1841-46. The relationship must have been distant because he doesn't show up in a genealogical search of the Peelles that Mother's sister, Marie, conducted more than fifty years ago. She was able to trace the Peelles back to 1689.

The prime minister was the second generation to receive the title of baronet. The fifth baronet married the actress-singer-comedienne Beatrice Lillie in 1920, so Mother thus added her as another adornment to the family tree, though not with the same enthusiasm as the prime minister.

Mother was intelligent but no intellectual. I think she feared anything that threatened her faith. She confined her reading pretty much to the local newspapers, the Catholic diocesan paper and such safe novels as A. J. Cronin's *The Keys of the Kingdom*, Franz Werfel's *The Song of Bernadette*, and Lloyd Douglas' *The Robe*. She loved Owen Francis Dudley's *The Masterful Monk*. She urged all of her children to read.

After Dad died Mother twice took jobs but neither worked out. One was to raise funds for Boys Town, the settlement for boys that Rev. Edward J. Flanagan founded near Omaha, Nebraska in 1922.

Mother had been sending checks and letters to Father Flanagan for a number of years. When she learned that he was to be in the city to give a talk, she invited him to dinner. In the course of the evening, the tall, thin priest with the Irish brogue suggested that Mother would be good at soliciting funds for Boys Town in small towns throughout the Middle West.

Why not, she thought; the kids are grown. Four of them were in service. Before going to work she rode a bus to Omaha to spend two weeks at Boys Town to learn more about the place. Two weeks away from home and the thought of riding buses all over the Midwest convinced her that she had made the wrong decision.

Her second venture was the *Indiana Catholic and Record*, the forerunner of *The Criterion*, the weekly newspaper of the Archdiocese of Indianapolis. I don't remember what her duties were on the paper but whatever they were they didn't last long. She left the office to walk home one evening shortly after she started work, stopping along the way to pick up groceries. When she didn't arrive home in time for supper, her brother Bob, who lived with us, and her son Bob both became alarmed. They went out looking for her. They were unsuccessful but at nine o'clock she showed up, tears streaming down her face. She and her sack of groceries had been caught in a rainstorm and she had gotten lost.

"This is it!" her brother declared. "No more working. You stay at home."

She quit the job but she didn't stay at home.

She was always eager to go. Never a scrupulous housekeeper, Mother thought a house was a place to live in, not a place to dazzle visitors. She much preferred getting out of the house.

World War II gave Mother her first real excuse to travel. By the time four of her children had left for service, she took her first major trip. She and my sister Virginia visited my brother Bill when he was an Army lieutenant stationed in New York City.

Twice she joined tour groups in Europe, but a bus trip to some town in Indiana was just as enticing.

On one Sunday morning she and Aunt Mary attended six am Mass so they could get an early start on a bus trip to Huntington. When she got home she discovered that she was short a twenty dollar bill and concluded that she had inadvertently dropped it in the collection basket. She quickly telephoned Father Cornelius Sweeney at the Cathedral to ask if a twenty dollar bill had shown up in the collection receipts. He confirmed that there was indeed one in the basket.

"I like you guys but not twenty dollars worth," she told him.

She retrieved the twenty dollars but two hours later had to make an embarrassing admission. The twenty dollar bill showed up in another purse. She handed the purloined bill back to Father Sweeney.

Aunt Mary was almost a second mother to us. Her door at Apartment 17 in Hampton Court was always open to us. If we happened to be there at lunchtime, we ate there. She and Mother chummed together.

Aunt Mary had a difficult childhood. She was raised by her grandparents who owned a grocery store in Haughville, a tough Irish neighborhood on the west side of the city. She recalled being awakened late at night and looking down from her bedroom window above the grocery store to see fights break out between the Irish laborers who lived and worked in the area. It was a common ending to a night of heavy drinking. She never forgot the sight of one man impaled on the iron picket fence in front of the house.

Aunt Mary almost never talked about those early years. She had more recent tragedies to deal with. Five years after her husband, our Uncle Harry, died, her son, Tom, a Naval pilot flew off an aircraft carrier in the Pacific in March 1945 and was shot down over Okinawa. Another daughter, Jane, died young, leaving eight young children. And a five-year-old granddaughter was drowned along with two other children in a swamp near their homes.

Aunt Mary was a survivor. She died in 1984 one week from her ninety-seventh birthday. She had borne eight children and left behind forty-two grandchildren and forty-three great-grandchildren. Even in her final year she could recall the birthdays of each of them.

By 1953 we had moved from Hampton Court to 3901 Park Avenue where mother lived until 1969. Mother spent the last years of her life at 6307 Evanston Avenue with Bill, a lifelong bachelor, and her brother Maurie Peelle. Sally and her family lived on the same block.

Mother had always relied on friends or Bill or other family members to drive her to the grocery store, to her meetings and weddings, funerals and wakes.

Wakes were rarely sad affairs for Mother. She was convinced that God, rather than a grave, had claimed the deceased. The visits to funeral homes to see off old friends were very often social affairs.

One night she showed up at three wakes in the same funeral home.

"She had a picnic," Bill recalled.

She was still writing letters at the age of eighty-six; the last one dated July 29, 1974, was sent to Sally who was vacationing at a summer home on Clear Lake in northern Indiana.

She spent the last months of her life in a nursing home across 86th Street from St. Vincent Hospital. She never complained about being there. Throughout her stay in the nursing home, one of her children or in-laws was there at mealtimes to help feed her.

Up to the end she was preaching table manners. She confided to me on one of those last days that she was fearful the nursing home people were going to evict her because she had lectured a tablemate. She explained that the man habitually got up from the table during meals, and wandered back and forth in the dining room. She said that it made her so nervous that during one meal she finally ordered him to sit down and eat his meal. The old gentleman complied, at least at that one sitting. Mother's fears of being evicted were groundless. The staff, I'm sure, approved.

She fell there one day and broke her hip. She never really recovered. Her brother Maurie finally joined her as a patient in the home but he lasted only two weeks before he died.

Mother died appropriately on Holy Thursday in the nursing home on March 27, 1975. She was eighty-seven. She had outlived her husband by thirty-six years, and her first child Nick by eight years.

The wake at Feeney-Hornak Mortuary on Easter Sunday brought together relatives, hundreds of her childrens' friends; politicians, including an ex-mayor or two; Legion of Mary colleagues who had accompanied her on calls made on troubled souls, and persons she had served with in clubs and organizations. A few strangers showed up throughout the evening mentioning only that she at one time had befriended them.

The gathering was more like a joyful and noisy reunion of family and friends.

After a funeral Mass at her parish church, Christ the King, Mother was buried next to her husband in Holy Cross Cemetery on the city's southside. Over the years people would come up to me and comment: "So you're Ag Connor's son. I remember your mother. She was a saint."

Did Anyone Know My Father?

I have often wondered if anyone ever really knew or understood my dad: not his children, not his co-workers, not even his wife. Dad was not a man who invited anyone to get close to him.

I'm told that before the Depression struck and before his salary was reduced drastically, he was a different man, more easygoing, more fun-loving. He became one of the millions of men in America whose lives were battered by the Depression. Life for him was never easy. And life with him wasn't always easy either.

His origins were humble. He was born in 1888 four months after his father, for whom he was named, had died at the age of thirty-eight. His father, Nicholas John Connor (born O'Connor), a railroader, died in Lafayette from the "acute rheumatism due to exposure" he contracted in the Army years before.

His mother, Margaret Foley Connor, the daughter of Irish immigrants, was unable to provide for all of her five children so Dad was raised by her sister in Lafayette.

He came to Indianapolis when he was about ten years old and probably lived with his mother and brothers and sister. He left school after the sixth grade; not uncommon for the Irish sons of laborers in those days. He never talked about his years as a child. Intelligent, ambitious and adept with numbers, Dad, I was told, could add a table of four numbers without laboriously adding each row singly.

By the time he married in 1912, he was cashier for International Harvester Company, a position he held for thirteen years. At one time he was transferred to St. John's, New Brunswick, a Canadian port north of Maine on the Bay of Fundy, noted for having tides as high as forty-five feet, the highest in the world.

Mother and their three children at the time—Nick, Bill and Bob—remained in Indianapolis. Dad stayed there less than a year. How different life would have turned out for all of them if they had moved to Canada.

After he returned to Indianapolis, he joined Holcomb & Hoke Manufacturing Company in 1919 as head bookkeeper. When the firm was started in 1913 it manufactured American Box Ball, a game similar to duck pins that was played in saloons and hotel lobbies. During Dad's years with the company the firm manufactured juke boxes and popcorn machines used in commercial establishments, as well as stokers that fed coal into furnaces.

Life appeared bright for him when he was named secretary of the company in 1929. But by 1932 the Depression had forced the company to cut his salary two-thirds overnight. It was a major blow and it forced the family to alter its lifestyle. At least he had a job.

Among Mother's effects was the draft of a letter she had written to Bishop Joseph Chartrand, thanking him for the financial assistance he had given the family so that Nick would be able to attend his sophomore year at the University of Notre Dame. The bishop had made a practice of aiding needy families with sons in college.

"Under ordinary circumstances," she wrote, "we would have been able to send Nick, but Mr. Connor's salary has been reduced until it is only a third of what it was, and rather than chloroform the rest of the children until the 'New Deal' has a chance to put us all on our feet again we had about decided to let him work for a year."

This would have been in the summer of 1933, the year Bishop Chartrand died.

Dad was up each morning at six am. He shaved his dark beard using a tube of Barbasol shave cream and Gillette Blue Blades in one of those heavy safety razors. He always dressed the same: a dark blue suit and vest, white shirt, dark tie, black shoes. He didn't own a sport coat or even sport shirts. His large midriff forced him to wear baggy one-piece BVDs and suspenders. He was out of the house by seven am, riding to work with co-workers in car pools because we never owned a car.

In effect, he was running Holcomb & Hoke because the owners frequently were absent. His son Bill, who worked summers there, said the factory workers feared him; that they speeded up their operations whenever Dad—with his grim visage—walked through the plant.

Many evenings he came home from work tired, worried and uncommunicative. We ate supper shortly after he arrived about 5:30. It was always the same, Mom calling, "Supper's on the table." About once a meal she chided one of us for our "boarding house reach," or "talking with your mouth full." If Dad was in one of his stern moods we got through the meal in silence, answering only when spoken to. Dad always seem to loosen up when we had guests, joking and kidding one of us. In the Depression years we had plenty of guests, usually a student-athlete that Bill or Bob brought home from Butler University. The boys liked the family atmosphere, but it was the home-cooked meals that attracted them.

It was a different table when Dad was not there, much freer and easier. When I was about thirteen I took a lot of ribbing during those meals from my brothers and the Butler athletes, especially if they had found out which movie star or entertainer I was in love with at the time. For awhile it was Peggy O'Neal, a cute little brunette who was one of the white hats in the Roller Derby that ran for several nights at Butler Fieldhouse. Peggy and Wes Aronson were the good guys; Jack Cummings and Dirty Gertie Scholl were the bad ones who viciously drove Peggy and Wes into the railings, or tried to trip them. As I remember, the four skaters on the steeply-banked track lazily skated until one of them took off in an attempt to lap the opposing skaters. The skaters furiously gave chase, driving their opponents into the railings. The chase might last ten minutes; then it ended with a score and the skaters, their hands on their hips, glided off the track, and substitutes replaced them. The noisy crowds always cheered for Peggy and Wes.

I reluctantly accepted the razzing I got for being enamored with Peggy O'Neal, but I finally balked one evening when the razzing turned to my current love, Sonja Henie, the ice skater turned movie star. Jerry Steiner, a star guard on the Butler basketball team, would not let up in needling me about Miss Henie. When I had enough, I fired a slice of bread covered with peanut butter across the table. It landed flush on Steiner's cheek and stuck there. Everyone but Mother laughed and it put a stop to Steiner's ribbing. It did a lot for my ego, too.

But it would never have happened if Dad had been sitting at the table. If that had been the case I might still be confined to my room.

Dad's post-dinner regimen was standard. He turned on the floor model radio and sank into his favorite chair to listen to Amos and Andy at seven o'clock, followed by one of the weekly shows of Jack Benny, Burns and Allen, or Fred Allen. Then he read *The Indianapolis News* until at some point, it sank into his lap and he napped for fifteen minutes.

Dad was no handyman around the house but we all understood he was the boss. He demonstrated that one Saturday afternoon when he came home from work. Mom greeted him at the door by telling him:

"Nick, there's a mouse on top of the kitchen cabinet."

"Where is he?" Dad asked.

Mother pointed near the ceiling. The little creature was perched on top of the cabinet a foot from the ceiling.

"I see him," Dad said. "I'll get him."

"We'd better get a mouse trap up there," Mom suggested.

"I'll take care of him," Dad said.

He stripped off his suit coat, grabbed a chair and climbed up on the counter top. It was a tight fit.

He ordered Mom to hand him the meat cleaver.

"You sure you want a meat cleaver?" she asked.

"Give me the cleaver," he said.

Armed with the cleaver, Dad went after his prey. The mouse darted back and forth as Dad repeatedly smashed down on the cabinet top. Chips flew to the kitchen floor.

I stared up at the battlefield, fascinated as Dad's face got redder as the chase went on. I knew that poor little mouse was a goner.

Mom began yelling, "Nick, you're ruining the cupboard...Nick you're going to fall...get down from there."

But the hunter was not to be deterred. He continued, inching along, chopping away.

When there wasn't much left of the rim of the cabinet, the mouse stopped for an instant. That did it. Down came the cleaver and the mouse separated into two pieces.

"I got the sonofabitch, Ag," he said.

Dad wasn't much for helping us with our homework. It was understood that homework and chores had to be done. We didn't often go to him for advice or guidance.

Dad may have been distant with his children but his family was his major interest. Little else engrossed him. Every penny he earned went to keeping us fed and housed. He rarely missed attending a game when his sons played football and basketball in high school and college.

He was an authority figure—at home, at work and at play. But as I look back on those early years most fathers were authority figures, their wives following the biblical injunction to be submissive to their husbands.

Dad's severity was punishment enough; he rarely struck us much more than a slap across the back of the head. If we got into trouble, smarted off to Mother, or balked about some chore, the sentence was always the same:

"Up to bed without your supper."

Sadly we would head upstairs. Mom usually showed up later with a plate of food, often, I'm sure, with a little prompting from Dad.

I don't ever remember our family eating a meal in a restaurant. But on Saturday afternoons Dad would sometimes take Mother to a neighborhood restaurant just to give her a break from all the children. Before leaving, though, she would have prepared the standard Saturday luncheon fare: hot dogs and baked beans.

If Dad determined that we were getting on his, or Mom's, nerves, he would give us each fifteen cents to attend a movie and buy a bar of candy.

Neither Mom nor Dad smoked or drank and the only social entertaining I can remember was when they came home from a high school athletic event with parents of some of the players. Dad had almost no friends outside the family.

As a young man he had joined the Knights of Columbus, but he had given that up by the time I came along. He was not a joiner, but he did belong to the old Hoosier Athletic Club, now the Turnverein apartments, at Ninth and Meridian streets, where he went each Tuesday evening to play handball.

Dad attacked athletics as he did life in general. Very competitive, he was vocal at sporting events, yelling at referees and umpires. On one of those Tuesday nights at the athletic club Bill went along and witnessed Dad and his handball opponent end up in a fist fight.

Both took off their glasses and were swinging wildly at each other. But Bill said neither landed more than a glancing blow.

He must have developed his large stomach early as an adult because I don't remember ever seeing him without it either in person or in any family photos. But in a 1906 photo with his Young Men's Institute (YMI) basketball teammates, he was the smallest member of the five-man team and appeared to weigh no more than 130 pounds. He was nineteen at the time, slim and handsome with a thick head of black hair that he never lost.

Despite his girth, Dad liked sports. He sometimes played golf on weekends, often at the old Speedway Golf Course. He didn't dress the part. He wore a regular white dress shirt and rolled up the sleeves.

For several years I was asked (ordered?) to caddy. Uncle Bob Peelle, Mother's brother, was often his playing partner. I never understood why he went along on those grim afternoons, but I guess it was an attempt to bring some harmony to the family.

Caddying for Dad was an ordeal for a twelve-year-old who knew almost nothing about golf etiquette. Dad had a routine of following each shot by muttering "shit," an apt comment. His swing never changed: a short, fast backswing and a lunge at the ball.

I usually tried to be as unobtrusive as possible so that I couldn't be accused of causing the errant shot. But one afternoon I made the mistake of handing him a two-iron instead of a putter on the green, a mistake compounded by having failed to locate his tee shot on the hole. As he lined up his putt, he realized I had given him the two-iron. He threw it off the green and tore into me about "not paying attention to what you're doing."

Chagrined, I headed down the fairway of the next hole to make sure I would be able to spot his tee shot. Walking down the fairway with me was Uncle Bob's caddy—one of those tough little Westsiders who worked as club caddies at the Speedway course.

"I wouldn't take that shit off that old bastard," the caddy remarked. When I told him he was my father, the caddy could only mutter "oh."

It was always a relief when the game ended. Dad soon mellowed and always treated me to a generous black cow in the clubhouse and then gave me a dollar for my efforts, the going rate for caddies.

Dad also liked vaudeville. He and Mom would ride the street-car downtown to attend the vaudeville at the Lyric Theater. Sometimes Dad would take one of us younger children along. I liked going because the Lyric usually showed one of those second-rate B movies before the vaudeville acts came on. I eagerly watched the movie while Dad snoozed.

I liked the tumblers and jugglers, the magic acts and the animal trainers, but I was often asleep when they brought on the dancing, country yokels and Abbott and Costello-type comedy acts.

Vaudeville was slowly dying in the thirties. After they stopped booking vaudeville here about the only live acts in the downtown theaters were burlesque at the Fox and Mutual theaters, both off-limits for people like our parents.

I never thought about it at the time, but I don't ever remember my parents embracing or showing any outward signs of affection to each other, and not much more to their children. In fact, few adults embraced publicly. Hugging came in with the flower children in the Sixties. Still Mom and Dad got along except on those nights when Dad sat down to balance the checkbook. Mother was not always careful about listing the check amounts and there was always some unexplained expense that caused Dad to lose his temper.

By the time we moved to Hampton Court, they slept in separate bedrooms. The arrangement may have been due to Dad's heart condition. He regularly took Digitalis, the common remedy for irregular hearts in those days.

His heart finally gave out on a clear fall afternoon in a place he loved: the Butler Bowl. The date was October 28, 1939. The occasion was a homecoming football game for Butler University. All of us were there along with seven thousand other fans to watch Butler play Washington University of St. Louis. It was Bob's senior year. Bill had graduated the prior spring. Just before the first quarter ended Bob, quarterback and team captain, threw a pass for a touchdown. Butler led 6 to 0.

A few minutes later Dad slumped in his chair. Mother thought he had reached down to pet a small dog that entered the box. When he didn't respond she called to Nick and Bill seated nearby to summon a doctor.

Virginia and I were watching the game with friends a few rows away. We saw some activity in the box but we were quickly ushered out of the stadium by Sally and some of her friends without knowing what had happened. We knew only that something had happened to Dad. The three of us boarded a bus for home.

After we left, some students carried Dad on a stretcher outside the gates. Dr. Hugh K. Thatcher, a deputy coroner at the game, pronounced death due to a heart attack. Mother, Bill and Nick knelt by his body and said prayers. Mother wanted to make sure that Bob was not told until the game ended. "His father would want him to finish the game," she said. So word went to the press box announcer that there was to be no announcement of his death. Bob was informed by the coach, Paul D. (Tony) Hinkle, after Bob had showered and dressed.

Mother arrived home ahead of the three of us. She told us then that he had died. At age fourteen I thought Dad was elderly but he was only fifty-one years old.

The days following are hazy. For three days relatives, friends and neighbors were in and out of the house day and night.

We held the wake in the dark and dingy Reynolds Mortuary, a block east of Hampton Court on Pennsylvania Street.

"He (the owner) needs the money," Mother declared. Reynolds' wife had been a schoolmate of Mother's.

The funeral at The Cathedral drew a large crowd. Friends of Bill and Bob from Butler acted as ushers and pallbearers. Dad was buried on a balmy Halloween morning in Holy Cross Cemetery on the city's southside.

J. I. Holcomb, a Butler trustee and a major benefactor of the university, happened to be in the stands when Dad died. In the lengthy page one story about his death in *The Indianapolis Star* the next morning, Holcomb, the president of Holcomb & Hoke, characterized Dad as "a tireless, conscientious, highly competent executive and one of the happiest family men I ever have known."

Mother commented years later that after Dad's funeral she never heard from J. I. Holcomb again.

Looking back on those days a half century later, I still recall the sense of relief tinged with guilt that I felt at his passing. The man I both loved and often dreaded was gone.

At the age of fourteen I had little understanding of the heavy burden he carried. Born without a father, raised by an aunt, overweight and stalked by a defective heart, Dad, especially in the last decade of his life, must have felt cheated by a Depression that robbed him of security and left him anxious and worried about caring for six children on a salary suddenly drastically reduced.

Perhaps it was the sudden lifting of parental control that gave me, a young teenager, the freedom I felt in the months after his death. But even more than that was the feeling that I no longer had to assess his moods to avoid his anger; that I no longer had to wonder what I must do to gain his approval.

In fairness, though, I discovered over the years that many fathers in those years ruled their families much as he did. Still, it was difficult for a boy to live with an authority figure like my Dad.

Agnes Peelle before her marriage to Nicholas J. Connor.

Nicholas J. Connor (left) and his Young Men's Institute basketball team pose for posterity in this 1906 shot.

Mother with Nick, her firstborn, in 1915.

Dad enjoys a laugh with his son Nick in 1916.

Bob and Maurie Peelle (second and third from left) with roller polo teammates in the Cyclorama rink in downtown Indianapolis about 1903. Note the No Smoking signs.

Certificate of Baptism

Church of

St. Joseph
Indianapolis, Ind.

This is to Certify

That _Agnes Peele Connor_
Child of _William Peele_
and _Margaret Fitzgibbons_
born in _Indianapolis, Ind._ on the
_18th_ day of _Dec._ 1887 was Baptized
on the _21st_ day of _January_ 1887
According to the Rite of the Roman Catholic Church
by the Rev. _Herman Alerding_
the Sponsors being _Della Fitzgibbons_
and _____ as appears from
the Baptismal Register of this Church.
Dated _June 11, 1947_

Rev. James H. Jansen Pastor

NO. 214 © D. P. MURPHY CO. NEW YORK

Official documentation that Mother joined the Catholic Church in 1888, even though the certificate misspelled Peelle.

Hampton Court

Aside from our genetic makeup, nothing forms us more than the time and place where we grew up.

For me and the rest of the Connors it was the 1930s and the place was Hampton Court a mile and half from downtown Indianapolis on Meridian Street, the city's major north-south artery.

It was a wonderful place for a child. About 250 persons, most of them young, lived in the twenty-nine large apartment units in the court. In 1934 when we moved in, there were at least two dozen children ages seven to fifteen. The Connors and most of the other tenants had few material goods, but we had caring parents, tolerant neighbors and all of those kids to play with.

We lived in Apartment 6. We filled it up. There were Dad and Mom, six of us children—Nick, Bill, Bob, Sally, Virginia and me—and we always had roomers and uncles living with us, as well.

Dad and Mom didn't select Hampton Court as a place to form their children's characters and personalities. They rented it because it had six bedrooms, reasonable rent and proximity to the church and schools we would be attending. Before then we had moved every couple of years from one three-bedroom rental house to another in the same neighborhood, but we stayed in Hampton Court for nineteen years.

The city had about 360,000 people in the thirties. It was pretty much a provincial city with few attractions, cultural or otherwise. Radio was still a novelty and it was years before television took over the nation's living rooms. There were no public parks or playgrounds or swimming pools within miles of Hampton Court, yet we survived and thrived.

Alleys and the large lawn that fronted the court were our main playgrounds. The lawn was bracketed on both ends by large trees and nondescript shrubbery. It was a time before pristine lawns became fashionable, so the residents didn't seem to care if the lawn took a beating from our baseball and touch football games, rope jumping, and games of tag and crack the whip. The curbing that separated the lawn from the driveway often served as a seating area for older residents on summer evenings.

Hampton Court was heavily Roman Catholic, principally because it was situated a block north of SS. Peter & Paul Cathedral and three Catholic schools grouped around the cathedral.

As Catholic children we had few doubts about our faith. If we didn't lie, or steal or cheat and tried to get along with our friends and neighbors we just knew we had a good chance of enjoying a full and happy life here and in the hereafter. If we didn't always measure up we could get a fresh start by going to confession at The Cathedral.

They talk today about the need for community. We had plenty of that in Hampton Court. It was white, middle class and mostly Roman Catholic.

Jean Osborne Gill, who grew up in the Court in those days, recalled sixty years later:

"I always felt so safe when I lived there because it was like having a big family that you could depend on. It was like a 'security blanket' had been put over the court and separated it from other neighborhoods."

The last one in at our apartment was supposed to lock the front door but it rarely got done. There was never much worth stealing anyway and the neighborhood was almost crime free. We walked the streets day or night without fear.

Most of that world is gone now. It was a time of innocence and naivete and joy for the young. For adults, trying to cope in the Depression, it was a time of worry, frustration and fear, but there were good times, too.

A few years before we moved in, the court had been home to some of the city's more affluent families. A few even housed servants on the third floors. By the time we arrived, the wealthier families had moved north into private homes.

Each unit had three floors and a full basement; six bedrooms, and two bathrooms, plus a toilet stool in the basement. Neither bathroom had a shower, and the tub in the third-floor bath had long ago lost its enamel so that bathers felt like they were sitting on sandpaper. No matter. To us it was luxurious having two bathrooms, especially in the mornings.

When the Court was built in 1924, the builders, acceding to prevailing superstition, numbered the twenty-nine apartments 1 to 30, skipping the number 13. The court had a horseshoe design; the apartments on the north and south wings were attached. Three other attached units made up the west end of the horseshoe. Four of the apartments, ours included, faced a walled terrace with concrete benches at either end.

The grounds of the court were lined with a privet hedge, about the only attempt at landscaping. A driveway at the front of the court curved around a large front lawn.

Hampton Court was built so solidly of red brick that we thought it would always be there, always be the same, but in a society that relies on change to propel it, neighborhoods come and go. Ours is gone. A motel that has changed owners and names at least three times now occupies the site of Hampton Court.

The four Connor boys slept under slanted ceilings in the two large bedrooms on the third floor, Nick and I in one of them, Bill and Bob in the other. Nick was twenty-one the year we moved in and I was nine. Bill was eighteen, Bob, sixteen. The walls of their room were covered with action photos of the world's sport figures they had brought home from *The Indianapolis Star*. The sports editor gave them unused wire service photos when they would show up at the paper to report on news and scores of high school games. We spent hours looking at those photos with kids in the neighborhood.

Sally, then eleven, and Virginia, eight, shared a room on the second floor; Dad and Mom each had a room and the fourth one usually was occupied by a roomer or one of two uncles who lived with us after Dad died.

Although the Depression was tearing the nation apart, there was no real sense of deprivation for us children. We had no idea what we were missing. Everyone faced the same shortages.

We had no reservations about walking into some of the apartments without knocking or ringing a doorbell, especially at Apartment 17 where Dad's older brother Harry lived with Aunt Mary and their eight children. They moved from the Eastside to Hampton Court a few months after we had moved in. Our cousins' ages pretty much paralleled ours, so it was almost like one big family living in two apartments. Uncle Harry was a detective on the Indianapolis

Police Department, a gentle, quiet man, certainly not a hard-boiled cop.

Their next-door neighbors were the Glaskas: Anna and Mary, John and Frank, all in their forties, none married. Theirs was an unusual arrangement. The women worked while John, who lost his sight as a young adult, and Frank, who had been gassed in World War I, stayed at home. We never saw much of Frank but John and his sisters always welcomed children. John sat in his darkened living room at all hours listening to the radio. He had lost his sight after graduating from the University of Notre Dame. The women were gentle and generous with children in the court.

Several apartments were leased by middle-aged women, mostly widows, who sub-leased rooms to young women who came from small towns in Indiana in search of jobs. Many were Catholics girls who got off the bus and showed up at The Cathedral seeking guidance on a place to live. The priests, in turn, often checked with residents of the court to see if a tenant had an empty bedroom. The priests called the place Vatican Court.

Tenants welcomed the girls because they had an excess of bedrooms and they needed money to pay the rent. In Apartment 1 Clarence and Florence Osborne and their three children, Jack, Jean and Mary Jane, lived on the third floor and rented the second floor to six roomers.

"That paid our rent of ninety dollars a month!" Jean recalled.

We had roomers living with us for several years. The going rate was ten dollars a week for room and board, which included breakfast and dinner.

It didn't take a roomer long to become part of our family. Some of them kept in touch with us years after they had left. Theresa Rabin, who migrated to Indianapolis in 1934 from St. Wendell, a small town in Southern Indiana, to work for the Internal Revenue Service, was still corresponding with members of the family more than fifty years after she moved out. We called her Trix. Exceptionally bright and a voracious reader, Trix sat up all night and read the entire 1,037 pages of *Gone With the Wind* in a single sitting, or, at least, that's what we were told. She lived with us off and on until 1941. She married an IRS agent, Edwin Kast, who died in 1993. Their daughter, Sheilah

Kast, is a network news reporter for ABC television, and their son Ken, a Ph.D. in mathematics science, specializing in topology.

Our first roomer was big Bob French, then a young sergeant in the regular Army. It was the mid-Thirties and he had been assigned from Fort Benning, Georgia to teach ROTC at Emmerich Manual Training High School. We thought Sarge immense at six feet, four inches. He wore size fifteen Army boots.

We got a surprise the first time we spotted him wearing short khaki pants and knee socks in the Army summer dress code of those days. When Dad spotted him coming up the walk, he remarked to Mother: "What's he doing out there in his underwear?" Bermuda shorts came later.

Bob said recently that living with us gave him a feeling of belonging to a family. He lived with us for a few months and then moved two doors away and joined the Drew family in Apartment 4. He said that Dan Drew induced him to move so that he could keep an eye on him because both of them were enamored with Jane Connor, one of our Hampton Court cousins. It must have worked; Dan married Jane.

One young woman who lived with us briefly became a source of embarrassment for Virginia when she was about eleven. Mother had befriended the woman and became her godmother when she joined the Catholic Church. She later became a nun but illness forced her to leave the order.

She stayed with us briefly after leaving the order. When she moved out, she left behind a pair of those heavy, black, sensible shoes that nuns wore with their ankle-length robes. They came in handy one day when Virginia needed a pair of shoes but there was no money to buy them. Mom stuffed paper into the toe of the shoes and sent Virginia trudging off to school. She stumbled along in them for a week until Mother scraped together enough money to buy her a pair of her own.

My sister still remembers "how embarrassed I was wearing those big black shoes."

It always seemed to be open house at Number 6. Kids were in and out all day, screen doors banging shut. An evening meal rarely passed that we didn't have a guest or two: some relative, a student, an athlete, or one of Mother's many female friends whom we called "Aunt Jess" or "Aunt May," though none of them were related to us. The leaves were never removed from the dining room table. There were always eight to ten people seated at the table in the evenings.

We were never certain who might drop in. Sunday afternoons, especially after a late Mass, people would show up. One fellow came in, ate Sunday dinner with us, thanked Mother and left. Bob asked Bill, "Who was that?"

"I don't know," Bill replied. "I thought he was a friend of yours."

Toni Connor, Bob's wife, recalled being in the living room one evening when a stranger walked in the front door and headed up the stairs. "Who's that?" someone asked. No one seemed to know—or care. A few minutes later he came down and walked out the front door without saying a word. Virginia said she was dressed in her slip and was in the bathroom with the door open when the man hit the landing. "Oops, sorry. Wrong apartment," he said and headed downstairs and out the front door.

Children liked our place because there was always a lot of activity, free food, and a generally relaxed atmosphere.

A friend remembered how free and easy kids ran through our apartment, so different from his house where his mother discouraged him from bringing friends home with him.

"Your Mom seemed always to have dozens of kids hanging out and eating her out of house and home! And she welcomed them! What a dame!"

When Cars Were Luxuries

The automobile had not yet ruled our lives in the thirties. Of the 250 residents in Hampton Court, fewer than a dozen owned cars. They parked them in rickety frame garages near the court's power plant.

Sometime in the late 1930s Nick became the first in our family to buy a car. He paid fifty dollars for an old green Franklin, a long, heavy car that had curtains on its windows. Franklins were no longer being built. In those days if you owned a Ford or Chevrolet, it was just that, a Ford or a Chevy; there were no models designated XII or ZTL. Automobiles were considered luxuries.

People in neighborhoods like ours didn't really need cars. All of our needs could be met within a short walking distance from Hampton Court. There were drug and grocery stores, a department store, banks, dry cleaners, laundry, furniture store, shoe repair shop, print shop, millinery shop, service stations, a Packard dealer, movie theaters, schools, churches, hospital, an art museum, bowling alleys, taverns, barber and beauty shops, a flower shop, restaurants and diners, an ice cream store, a fire station, at least six funeral homes, plus doctors, dentists, jewelers, a watchmaker, a cobbler, tailor, and a bookie.

The stores were closed on Sundays. Almost none of the stores are there today. Parking lots, service stations and empty lots occupy the sites.

Mother liked shopping in Sablowski's department store, the Wal-Mart of the thirties. It was located in a one-story building behind Hampton Court on Illinois Street. Low prices lured her into the store. The goods were as low as the prices. She shopped for bargains in essentials: underwear, socks, towels, curtains.

We liked to peek into Kelso's jewelry shop next door, mainly to watch old Mr. Kelso with his long white beard squinting into the workings of someone's watch. He seemed a mysterious figure from some village in the Alps.

If we couldn't find what we needed in the neighborhood shops, it was no trouble getting downtown. Buses operated on Meridian Street; streetcars that rocked from side to side ran on Illinois Street one street behind us, and silent trackless trolleys operated on Pennsylvania one street east of Meridian. Bus rides cost a dime, streetcars and trackless trolleys seven cents or four tokens for a quarter, transfers two cents. People went downtown to work, to shop at the major department stores—Blocks, Ayres, Wassons, Sears, Strauss and Charlie Mayer—or to attend movies, vaudeville or stage shows in one of the nine downtown theaters.

Even though Broad Ripple was annexed to the city in 1922, a trip there by streetcar seemed like an all-day venture. We tagged along when Mother went there to visit Rose Stout, one of her many friends that we called aunts, though there was no blood relationship.

The automakers in Detroit managed to convince American cities that streetcars and trackless trolleys were archaic methods of transportation, so Indianapolis retired its last streetcar in 1953 and its last trolley in 1957. Ironically, streetcars remain as the principal form of transportation in many European cities.

There may not have been many cars in our neighborhood but the city still liked to brag that forty-four different makes of cars, including Duesenberg, Stutz and Marmon, were produced in Indianapolis in the decade before 1917.

Women seldom drove cars before 1932 because the cars had to be cranked before they would start. The cranks often kicked back, sometimes resulting in a broken arm for the cranker. In those early cars, the front seats had to be removed so gasoline could be pumped into the tank. With each gallon, the pump would ring a bell. It was not uncommon to find cars jacked up in the winter months to save the tires from wear. An out-of-town trip always carried the risk of blowouts of tires.

Now and then we'd spot an electric car driven by some stout matron on her way to the Propylaeum on Delaware Street. We knew that meant old money.

Generally, though, our neighborhood was one of middle-class renters: substantial people who took public transportation to their jobs as bookkeepers, salesmen, store managers and salaried workers. They, in turn, produced a generation of physicians, lawyers, merchants, priests, politicians, scientists, accountants and engineers, even a few millionaires, and its share of thieves and drunks.

The neighborhood was in another of Meridian Street's transitional stages. At the turn of the century the street south of 16th Street was lined with mansions erected by the city's wealthy leaders. They were three-story structures; the third floors sometimes served as ballrooms or servants' quarters. A few were still around in the 1930s but the trees lining the streets were gone and many of the homes had been converted into offices. The original owners had long since moved north beyond 38th Street.

The Red Cross in 1942 moved into one of those old mansions at 1126 North Meridian, which was built in 1863 by William S. Hubbard, one of the city's pioneers. The Children's Museum, in those days little more than a collection of stuffed birds and animals and butterfly displays, occupied a house built in 1873 at 1150 North Meridian. The house was razed in 1948 after the museum moved north to 30th Street on Meridian, where it later expanded into new quarters and became one of the city's major attractions.

One of the few houses that remained—this one stood until 1979—was the Sullivan House across Meridian Street from the court. The former residence of two-time mayor Reginald Sullivan, it became Jackie's Lounge, one of those dark and dreary two-level gin joints that took over old houses after World War II.

Charles Warren Fairbanks moved into a home at 1522 North Meridian in 1903—the year before he was elected Theodore Roosevelt's vice-president. A senator at the time, he was chosen with little enthusiasm but as Roosevelt observed, "who in the name of Heaven else is there?" Roosevelt was a guest at the house in 1907, as was President William Howard Taft in 1911.

Long before Hampton Court was built, Fairbanks had left the area and erected a mansion far out at 30th and Meridian; now the home of the Indianapolis Life Insurance Company. Mother said Fairbanks referred to the house as his "little cottage."

Tudor Hall, the school for daughters of the city's rich and famous, was located at 16th and Meridian until 1917 when it, too, moved north to 32nd and Meridian streets.

While the rich and famous were moving north to grand quarters, we were moving, too. In fact, we moved about every two years but it was from one rental house to another, usually a block or two north or south of 16th Street. I never knew why we moved; most of the houses looked the same. The single units were two-story frame houses with a brick front porch, three and four bedrooms with a single bathroom on the second floor: a library, living room, dining room and kitchen on the first floor. The doubles had three bedrooms and a bath on the second floor; the front porch was divided by a low brick wall. I don't remember any of the houses having finished basements; some even had dirt floors. They housed massive coal-burning furnaces and washtubs where women scrubbed the week's laundry on washboards each Monday.

Sometime in the 1970s Bill compiled a list of the houses the family had occupied since Dad and Mom had married and moved into their first house at 2347 North Delaware. By the time we moved into Hampton Court, we had lived in eight houses, all within a half-mile radius. Four of them are still standing, though two of them just barely.

We children weren't told why we kept moving, but it may have been because the landlords thought a family of six children and a dog were more than their property could handle. At least that was the reason why we moved from 1840 North Talbot Street in 1928. The landlord persuaded us to move the day after supper was interrupted by the dining room ceiling crashing down on the table. Mom insisted it was due to poor workmanship, but the owner countered that the plaster work had held up for thirty-five years.

Mom didn't tell the landlord that the bedroom above the dining room was occupied by Bob and Bill, ages ten and twelve. For weeks they and their friends had been using their beds as trampolines, despite Mother's repeated orders to "stop jumping on the beds."

When we moved, we left behind a grassless backyard and a basketball goal nailed to the garage. About the only landscaping at any of those houses were some petunias and lillies of the valley that Mother planted around the foundation of the house. I do recall there were two cherry trees in the back yard of the house at 1731 North Pennsylvania Street. We were assigned to pick the cherries each summer, but there were so many non-Connor pickers that Mother never seemed to end up with enough cherries for more than two pies.

All of the blocks in the neighborhood were bisected by alleys, most of which were lined with sagging garages and trash and garbage

containers but they served nicely as our playgrounds and shortcuts
to friends' houses. Some of them had been paved with bricks at one
time. Getting cars down the bumpy alleys and into tiny garages took
skill.

Author Lewis Mumford, an architectural and urban critic, spoke
for us when he wrote: "More often than not, I would prefer to walk
in the rear alley, precisely for all those little hints of life, activity, and
transition which the placid visual arts of suburbia did their best to
suppress or politely disguise."

A house the family rented at 1719 North Delaware in 1921 had
been occupied earlier by mother's sister Marie and her husband, Will
Seaton. While they were vacationing in Florida one winter, the water
pipes on the second floor froze and burst. Water flowed through the
house for two weeks, producing ice a foot thick. Bill said that from
then on "the house retained the faint odor of a privy."

Slowly my old neighborhood began crumbling after the end of
World War II. The few mansion-sized houses still standing were converted into four and six-unit apartments to capitalize on the demand
for housing from returning veterans. There were years in the 1960s
when old houses in the neighborhood became targets of bricks and
molotov cocktails. Meridian Street was spared mainly because it had
become a home to respectable businesses. Other streets in the area,
though, took on seedy looks. It was painful to drive through the area;
it was as though your birthright had been stripped from you. In time
empty lots outnumbered houses on a block.

The deterioration slowed beginning in the late 1970s. Some of
the older residents who had stayed on put a fresh coat of paint on
their houses and spruced up their lawns and flower beds—encouraged by neighborhood organizations interested in preservation. In
time the yuppies arrived, spending their nights and weekends restor-
ing the two and three-story houses with their solid oak stairways and
leaded windows. It wasn't the same as it was growing up there but it
was a lot less painful to drive through the old neighborhood.

This was the area in the 1930s and forties where we played kick
the can in the alleys, shot baskets in dusty backyards, played penny-
ante poker for hours next to coal bins in basements; talked of growing up and owning Chevy coupes with rumble seats, and gathered in

houses for clandestine postoffice parties, the pretext being some female's thirteenth birthday. It was about that time that the boys began describing the pubescent girls as "stacked." Mothers commented that they had "nice figures."

The sights and sounds stay with me yet: car horns tooting or "ahoogahing," bicycle bells jingling, firecrackers going off beginning at dawn on July 4th, winter muffled by snow as laughing children rushed by on sleds, open-bed trucks selling fresh fruit and vegetables to housewives, summertime hawkers yelling, "strawwberrriees, strawwberrriees, strawberries," junkmen hollering their pleas for "rags and old iron."

The junkmen had heavy, handmade carts riding on old tires mounted on large wheels. They pushed them by standing between the cart and a wooden bar jutting out from the cart. I envied those junkmen because they always seemed to have interesting stuff. I dreamed of owning a pickup truck to haul the junk I scavenged from neighbors' trash; old chairs, broken rakes, discarded motors, items I was certain could be reclaimed with a little effort.

In addition to the junk I carted home, Virginia and I collected the neighbors's unwanted mail, storing it in the library table—one drawer for Virginia, one for me.

In our pre-school years, Virginia and I loved carrying Mother's old purses jammed with our possessions. A few short years later, though, after we had been schooled that boys didn't carry purses, the two of us got in trouble for taunting and beating up two younger neighbor boys caught carrying purses. They were the same two boys who regularly called us "cat lickers."

They once begged us for some of the caramels we were eating, so Virginia and I carefully carved a bar of caramel-colored Fels Naptha soap into the shape of candy and gave it to them. I can still see the look on their faces as they hungrily stuffed the pieces into their mouths. We didn't see much of them after that.

That wasn't as serious—nor did it compare with the scolding we received—for tying a neighbor kid to a post and carrying out a mock Indian burning ritual. Even without fire, the prank terrified the kid and infuriated his mother.

One of summer's drawbacks was house flies hovering around garbage cans on back porches. There was a fly swatter in every kitchen, and hanging from the ceilings were long strips of sticky paper dotted with dead flies.

By the age of twelve we were spending summer afternoons at the Cinema Theater on 16th Street taking in double features, one of them often starring the Dead End Kids, a Popeye cartoon, and a Movietone newsreel all for a dime. In the evenings we crossed Meridian Street to buy four-dipper ice cream cones for a nickel at Tomkins Ice Cream store. Teenagers sipped cherry cokes at drug store soda fountains. Sally and her friends spent lazy afternoons walking downtown with friends to buy a large pickle at Weiss' delicatessen for a nickel.

She and other friends in the seventh and eighth grades—boys and girls—would meet and attend the Cinema for a movie on Sunday afternoons, then head for the Cathedral for mandatory vespers service.

"But we always split up before we got to church," she said. "The boys would go in one door and we girls in another. We never wanted the sisters to know we had been together."

The multi-breed dogs that were always around when we were young usually were there because my Uncle Tommy would pick up a mutt and bring it as a gift to the kids. Mother hated having them because it always fell to her see that they got housebroken, despite the promises of her children that they would be responsible for the training and cleanup duties.

One of the mutts was an ugly little black and white, short-haired terrier we called Siggy. One day Siggy failed to zig and was run over by a car in front of the house. Virginia, about six at the time, took Siggy's death with equanimity. She told the mourners: "It was he own fault. He did it he self."

It was a time when salesmen peddling dish rags, shoe laces, hairpins and red bandanas showed up at the front door every few months; when the tall, orange-painted Povinelli truck made semi-annual trips to the neighborhood to sharpen knives and scissors; when the mailman delivered mail twice a day, and the milkman placed quart bottles of milk (the top third cream) in milk boxes on back porches.

Housewives placed cards in front windows signaling to the iceman that they wanted twenty-five or fifty or one-hundred-pound blocks of ice for their iceboxes. The Polar Icemen used tongs to bring the twenty-five and fifty-pound hunks of ice to the house. They carried the one-hundred-pound blocks on burlap rugs over their shoulder, then deposited the blocks at the top of the ice box. The drip pan under the ice box had to be empted daily. In winter coal was carted in a wheelbarrow from a truck in the street and dumped down a chute into the basement.

Downtown Indianapolis had its charms but its streets were littered with trash and the buildings were darkened from soot. It was decades before the city and businesses dressed up the green spaces downtown with flower beds and attractive landscaping.

Then as now Monument Circle was the downtown's principal attraction. In the thirties the ornate English Hotel and Opera House sat on the northwest quadrant; the northeast quadrant was anchored by Christ Church Cathedral. The new Circle Tower sat proudly on the southeast quadrant next to the Circle Theatre movie house. Across Meridian Street on the southwest sector was the H. P. Wasson department store. Every high school kid at one time or another had to trudge the steps to the top of the Soldiers and Sailors Monument, at that time the downtown's highest building.

One of the major cultural attractions in our neighborhood was the Herron Art Institute and Museum at 16th and Pennsylvania streets. It was founded in 1902 with a $200,000 bequest by John Herron, who had inherited a family fortune. Many of Indiana's artists studied, taught and exhibited their work in the art galleries.

We didn't associate with the art students who came from other parts of the city and state. They seemed so purposeful and distant hauling their portfolios into the building. On slow summer days we would roam through the museum, even though the place seemed so eerily quiet and the attendants treated us with suspicion, and rightly so.

Late one July night in 1938 two of Bob's friends escaped the eyes of the guard and managed to provide some excitement the following afternoon. Not long before a sculpture of an enormous horse and rider had been unveiled on the mall before a crowd of officials and art lovers. On the morning I'm referring to in July, guests to the museum who came to see the wonderful horse were startled by a large mound of horse manure beneath the horse's rear quarters.

One of the perpetrators spent twenty years as a cop on the Indianapolis Police Department; the other spent his adult life selling baby foods.

The Optimistic Twenties

In 1925, the year I was born, Indianapolis and the rest of the country was enjoying itself. The economy was booming. Radio and "talkies" at the movies were providing inexpensive entertainment. A new weekly news magazine, *Time*, was opening up the world for Americans with its brash and breezy style. The rich and not-so-rich were buying automobiles, and in Indianapolis families were moving into spendid new homes north of 38th Street.

Life was promising for the Connors, as well. Dad had been named secretary of Holcomb & Hoke Manufacturing Company, earning a respectable salary. His brother Arthur, whom we kids called Uncle Tommy, had started his own printing company, Centennial Press.

Our family took its final form in the twenties. Sally arrived in 1923, and Virginia a year after I was born. We joined Nick, who was born in 1913; Bill born in 1916, and Bob in 1918.

By the end of the twenties, the city had taken on a new look. Three of the city's major architectural attractions downtown were built in the first quarter of the century. The first to open had been the Federal Building in 1905. The Italian Renaissance building had beautiful marble floors and walls, an arched ceiling of mosaics, with self-supporting circular stairways of marble on the east and west ends. The Central Library built in the Greek Revival style opened in 1917, and the Scottish Rite Cathedral, an unusual combination of Gothic and Tudor styles, opened its door in 1929. Those structures, along with the Classical Revival-styled World War Memorial (completed in 1927), the American Legion headquarters, and two block-square parks provided an impressive stretch of public structures that today are still the city's major downtown treasures.

It was in the twenties that the three youngest Connors received nicknames. Virginia was saddled with the name Tubby. Nick dubbed me Bozo after a wrestler with that name who had performed in the city. Nicknames are difficult to jettison. Virginia fought hers and finally won the battle in high school. I never completely lost mine, though I did manage to drop the last syllable before I reached my teens. Later Bill gave me another appellation after I had affected a

41

French accent one summer, referring to me as Pierre Bozo, which he shortened to Pierre, the name he called me until he died.

Sally was christened Mary Margaret—probably in honor of her two grandmothers named Margaret—but she was called Sally almost from birth, she believes because Dad was raised by Sally Hannegan, her great-aunt. Virginia contests that version. She insists that Dad came home one day singing, "I Wonder What's Become of Sally?" and his daughter, perched on the mantle, looked down and said, "Here I am."

A year after Virginia was born, a new Cathedral High School opened at 14th and Meridian streets. It became a major influence on the family until I graduated from there in 1943. The Butler Fieldhouse on the new campus of Butler University also opened in 1927. It was one of the largest fieldhouses in the nation with 14,000 seats. Butler's basketball team became national champions a year later. Our family spent thousands of hours over the years watching Butler basketball teams and other events in the cavernous fieldhouse. There was a mystique about the place, the home of so many great moments in sports.

The city had every reason to be optimistic by that time. The population in 1930 had grown to 364,000. New parks and boulevards were created. Garfield Park on the Southside featured a pagoda and elaborate sunken gardens. White River, Pogue's Run, Pleasant Run and Fall Creek all became lined with parkways, thanks to the vision of George Edward Kessler, a nationally recognized landscape architect and consultant on city planning. Kessler Boulevard also was constructed in the 1920s.

Indianapolis Municipal Airport was created in 1928 when the city purchased 947 acres west of the city. It grew slowly. Its terminal even during World War II was nothing more than a small building topped by a control tower.

My cousin Jim sold candy and popcorn at the airport in the lobby of the terminal one year in high school. The stand was owned by gruff Leo Hurley, who supplied the food for airline passengers. The job was something of a bonus for Jim. At that time he was dating Hurley's pretty daughter, Margaret.

Radio was a novelty in the early twenties. The city's first radio station—WLK, a 250-watt station—went on the air in 1921, followed by WOH, but both closed within a year. Noble Watson, who started WOH, came back and opened WBBO and WKBF, which became WIRE in 1935. We bought one of those floor radios that looked like a piece of fancy furniture.

It wasn't long after they started producing full-length movies that Indianapolis began to get some of the seventy movie theaters it would have at its height. The Circle Theater opened in 1916. Some of the major movie houses opened in the twenties: the Loews Palace in 1921, A. C. Zaring's Egyptian Theater at Fall Creek and Central Avenue in 1925, and the Indiana Theater and the Indiana Roof in 1927.

Indianapolis residents were generally hard working, conservative, and isolationist. There were pockets of Irish, Italian and Germans scattered throughout the city. The Westside had immigrants from Eastern Europe—Slovenes, Croats, Poles, Serbs and Hungarians—but the city, and the rest of the state, was largely native-born white Protestants.

It may have been the predominance of white Protestants that accounted for the strength of the Ku Klux Klan; an estimated half million Hoosiers were members in 1924, six million nationwide. The Klan's targets were Catholics, Jews and blacks. Catholics were regarded as cheap labor. Many advertisements for workers carried the proviso: "No Irish Need Apply."

The extent of the Klan's influence had to have affected our parents and relatives, but I can't recall much talk about it when I was growing up. If anything, they ridiculed the Klansmen who paraded in their white hoods and robes past Catholic churches and synagogues in silent warnings. There were tales about young Catholic youths disrupting parades by singling off the last rows of Klan parades and beating up the Klansmen, but I never knew of anyone who participated.

Aside from the disgrace that the Klan brought on the state, the 1920s were years of optimism and hope for Hoosiers, including Catholics and especially the Connors.

That optimism and hope didn't last long.

Those Pessimistic Thirties

As the song has it, what a difference a day makes.

The day was October 29, 1929. It changed all of our lives. Optimistic America turned to Pessimistic America in the days and years that followed the stock market crash on that October day. Fear came first; then a gradual sense over the next decade that the good times would never return.

While that monumental upheaval of the 1930s made life difficult for adults, I can't remember feeling particularly deprived. My three older brothers, who grew up in the twenties, could look back wistfully on the good times, especially at Christmas when the number and quality of the gifts around the tree didn't compare to that of earlier Christmases. But it was different for Sally and Virginia and me. We grew up in the thirties. You don't miss something you never had or never expected to receive.

If there were complaints we were brought into line by one of Mother's aphorisms:

"Money doesn't grow on trees"..."beggars can't be choosers" or the standard mealtime remark: "If you always have it this good you'll never starve."

True enough. We never did starve, never went hungry. We always seemed to have enough food for whoever showed up. We ate a lot of macaroni and cheese, gravy bread, meatloafs, vegetable soups and chili con carne. Mother bought oleomargarine that looked like lard until she transformed it into "butter" with coloring.

We ate on dishes that didn't match and drank tap water from crystal goblets that Mom and Dad had received as wedding gifts twenty years earlier. Dessert, if there was any, likely would be rice pudding, tapioca or jello.

But we had it better than the Westsider who recalled those days, topping everyone's stories of woe by remarking, "We were so poor that we ate cereal with a fork so we could save the milk."

True, we and others in our neighborhood got along as best we could. There were always other children worse off than we were. We stuck cardboard in our shoes when the leather sole wore through. The familiar clap-clap on the sidewalk meant the sole of somebody's shoe had pulled free.

The Depression forced Nick to drop out of the University of Notre Dame after two years. There wasn't money to pay the tuition, so Nick got a job with the Treasury Department to help support himself and the family. By then Dad's salary as secretary of Holcomb & Hoke Manufacturing Company had been decimated.

There were no weekly allowances, no candy at home, no Coca Cola or Royal Crown Cola in the ice boxes. We made do. Crooked teeth stayed crooked. We drank water, rather than milk, at our meals. Mother melted soap scraps and fashioned them into bars of soap.

And of course amusements were restricted.

Few families we knew took summer vacations. In fact, I don't remember Dad ever taking time off from work. He would have been uncomfortable staying around the house. He was not a handyman.

We were no different from other families. The Depression came on so quickly. The economy had boomed throughout the twenties and suddenly business came to a standstill. Banks, savings and loans, mortgage companies and insurance companies failed, shops were boarded up, factories wound down; men lost their jobs. And because few women worked outside the home, there was no second income to help support a family. Families had to adjust, doing without former comforts they had enjoyed.

One summer I attended Boy Scout camp for a week. It cost seven dollars. It was a wonderful place for a boy, and I had hoped that I would be able to stay a second week, but Mother said it was either that or a new suit which she said I needed. I had no interest in the clothes, but I was dutiful and came home from camp and got the suit.

There was no talk of men retiring; they worked until they wore out or died. And when they wore out there was no health insurance.

Even the 500-Mile Race at the Indianapolis Motor Speedway was in jeopardy. There was talk of dropping the race until the economy improved. In 1933 the winner, Louie Meyer, collected only $18,000 in Speedway and lap prize money, about a third of what Billy Arnold won in 1930.

When the Depression hit Indianapolis, building virtually stopped and stayed dormant until after World War II. The city took on a seedy look. Even Woodruff Place and Irvington—thirty years earlier two of the city's showcase residential areas—began to shows signs of decline. Woodruff Place on the near Eastside was no longer the community that Booth Tarkington used as the setting for his Pulitzer Prize (1919) novel, *The Magnificent Ambersons*. Many of the large, three-story homes were being turned into rooming houses and apartments.

Government was about the only entity doing any building. A Veterans Administration Hospital opened on Cold Spring Road; a state library went up downtown; the Naval Reserve Armory was built; Lockefield Gardens, the city's first Federal housing project designed for black families, opened, and the Indiana University Medical Center was expanded. The Circle Tower on Monument Circle was completed in 1930. It was the last of the tall downtown buildings erected until the 1950s.

Bill said of those days that the difference between being rich and poor was a five-dollar bill.

Those were the years when bus drivers and teachers earned $1,300 a year, a double bed and mattress cost twenty-five dollars, and a family could buy an eight-piece dining room set for forty-five dollars. Free dish towels came with a large box of soap powder; an office visit to a physician cost $1, and stamps cost two cents with a penny buying a postcard stamp. Bank Nights with prize moneys at the movies were a big attraction. On other nights free dishes were given out. A young couple could supply themselves with a service for eight just by going to the movies once a week.

Plastic credit cards were in the future. People bought furniture and appliances on the monthly installment plan, or put them in "layaway" until they could save enough money to pay for them.

Nick spent eight days in St. Vincent Hospital in 1935 to undergo an appendectomy. The total hospital bill was $53.25; broken down as $3.60 per day for the room, the operating room fee was $15, anesthesia was $4.50, laboratory cost was $3, plus $2.05 for incidentals.

In those days there were some seventy movie houses in the city, nine of them downtown. We looked forward to Sunday afternoons when we were took our dimes and headed for one of the theaters in the neighborhood: the Talbot, Cinema, Stratford or St. Clair. For that dime we could count on four hours of entertainment—a double feature, cartoons and a newsreel. We saw inspiring films: *Captains Courageous, Goodbye, Mr. Chips, Mr. Deeds Goes to Town, David Copperfield, Mutiny on the Bounty, A Tale of Two Cities, Lost Horizon*, and family films like the *Andy Hardy* series with Mickey Rooney and Judy Garland, *Snow White and the Seven Dwarfs* and *The Wizard of Oz*, one that I must have seen a dozen times. We liked the second features—the B movies with actors like Chester Morris, Stu Irwin and the Dead End Kids —almost as much as the main attractions.

Parents didn't have to worry about the content of the movies because the Legion of Decency was rating them. There were no naked partners grappling on beds. The thrill seekers sneaked into the seedy Cozy Theater downtown. Its films advertised in the newspapers carried the Adults Only warning above such titillating titles as *How to Undress in Front of Your Husband, Sally Rand's Wonder Ranch, How to Take a Bath, Behind the Scenes in Model Schools.*" And there were the burlesque houses—Fox and Mutual—but they, too, were off limits to us.

A lot of the ballads of the thirties are still being recorded: "I've Got You Under My Skin," "Smoke Gets In Your Eyes," "I Can't Get Started," "These Foolish Things," A Foggy Day," "Where or When," "Our Love Is Here to Stay." Not a "baby, baby, baby" in the bunch.

Comics in *The Indianapolis Star* even in those days included "Blondie" and "Henry," as well as such standbys as "Joe Palooka," "Jiggs," "Mickey Finn," "Big Chief Wahoo" (later to evolve into "Steve Roper"), "Tillie the Toiler" and "Dixie Dugan."

We made regular bus trips to the Butler Fieldhouse to watch Butler basketball games but it was the six-day bicycle races and the roller derbies staged in the fieldhouse that excited us. Somehow there were always free passes available. On warm summer nights Bill and Bob and their friends would pool their change and come up with enough to buy two gallons of gasoline to get a family car to the North Pole, a drive-in at 5600 North Illinois Street where high school and college-age boys and girls congregated. They usually had enough money to purchase a Coke apiece. Occasionally I got to tag along.

Talk was cheap in the Depression, so there was a lot of it. People sat around kitchen tables and listened to Father Charles Coughlin rant in Sunday afternoon radio broadcasts about the need to put America first; shook their heads over the latest antics of the Louisiana rabble rouser Huey Long, listened to FDR's fireside chats, talked of jobs and the New Deal, and argued about labor unions and big business.

There was talk about bread lines and soup kitchens and hobo camps on the radio and in newsreels but they were always in some other part of the country. All we saw were occasional hoboes at the back door.

One Saturday afternoon Dad stormed in from the alley to demand which of his children had defaced the garage with mysterious chalk marks. His anger evaporated after Mom explained that the children didn't make the marks; that they were made by hoboes as a way of informing fellow hoboes they could expect a meal at our house.

Like the movies, sports helped people forget their troubles. We listened to heavyweight boxing matches on the radio when Joe Louis was in his prime, hoping that some white boxer would come along and whip him, later viewing the Brown Bomber as a hero, especially after he knocked out the German, Max Schmeling, in his rematch to regain the title. On Saturday afternoons we stretched out on living room floors to listen to the radio broadcasts of Notre Dame football games.

The string of bold bank robberies by John Dillinger, a punk from Mooresville, and his companions armed with machine guns provided some diversion and even a little admiration but our hero wasn't Dillinger; it was Melvin Purvis, the Federal agent who chased Dillinger and his gang.

The nuns in the grade school tried to do their part to lift the spirits of hard-pressed parents. I, and presumably all of the other children in the class, brought home a note from school one afternoon. I found it fifty years later in a box of school notes and report cards Mother had saved.

"The Depression is almost over," I had penciled in my best

Palmer Method on flimsy lined paper: "There will soon be plenty of work and money again. Our Holy Father the Pope said so."

But alas, His Holiness, was a bit premature. The note was written in 1932.

Playing Without Playgrounds

There were no parks or playgrounds, swimming pools or community centers within miles of Hampton Court, but it didn't matter. We found ways to enjoy life.

We spent hours in the basement playing one-on-one basketball games, using a tennis ball and small baskets made out of coat hangers attached to small boards wired to two steel supports. When we tired of that we set up the ping pong table and played round-robin tourneys, using sandpaper-covered paddles.

Basements in Hampton Court were the scene of many parties. Sally and some of her friends worked several days painting the walls of the basement white in preparation for a party for her high school friends. The night of the party, each of her guests got the idea of signing their names on the walls. They found a can of black paint and by party's end the walls were covered with names and comments. The walls stayed that way until we moved out a dozen years later.

It was a time before Little Leagues but we usually found a half dozen boys and girls to get a baseball game on the lawn of Hampton Court or behind Cathedral High School.

We all had our favorite baseball players. They weren't Yankees or Cardinals, either. They were Indianapolis Indians, who played other American Association teams in what was then known as Perry Stadium on West 16th Street. It later became Victory Field and finally Bush Stadium, named after the city's best known professional baseball player, Owen Bush.

We read Nancy Drew and Hardy Boys mysteries, Big Little Books that featured stories about Flash Gordon, Buck Rogers and Dan Dunn, Secret Operative. As I recall, Big Little Books cost a dime. They were fat but measured about three and a half by four and a half inches, fitting nicely in a boy's back pocket. There were hundreds of them in the late 1930s but I can't recall seeing any after the war.

Later I would isolate myself in my bed on the third floor and devour Jack London novels. But my favorite book was Richard Halliburton's *The Royal Road to Romance*. His exploits—climbing the

Matterhorn or swimming the Hellespont as Lord Byron had done a century earlier—took me to strange and exciting places.

We always had magazines around the house—*Liberty, Colliers, Saturday Evening Post* or *Ladies Home Journal*— usually because some newspaper carrier was selling subscriptions at rock-bottom prices to gain a trip to Chicago or Washington, D. C.

We worked at coming up with "knock, knock" jokes and dreaming about trips we would take when we reached age sixteen—generally to California, and on bicycles at that. We mailed off Wheaties box tops for badges, binoculars, model airplanes and other cheap toys. We met the mailman morning and afternoon hoping he would be delivering our prizes.

On summer days the boys squeezed around an old table next to the coal furnace in Baltz's basement and played penny-ante poker for hours in the dark, dreary cellar. It was a successful day if you came home fifteen cents ahead; devastating if you lost that much. Fifteen cents would buy three Baby Ruth candy bars.

On summer evenings we dashed out after doing the dishes to play catch in the yard at the front of the court, while the girls jumped rope or played hop scotch on the driveway. The boys and girls played hide and seek. We knew we were coming of age when two of the boys found a hiding spot in a tree just outside one of the girl's second-foor bedrooms. They lost interest in the game we were playing and remained in the tree.

Without air conditioning, people sat on front porches on hot summer nights, hoping for a breeze. Sometimes they would bring out an electric fan and hook it up inside with an extension cord. Some of the men sat on swings in their undershirts, sipping lemonade, while their children, unfazed by the heat, raced around the yards playing tag or hide-and-seek.

We had no front porches at Hampton Court, so the adults— mostly young men and women—spent hours in the evening sitting on the curbing around the driveway in the front of the court. We youngsters played our games until one of the adults suggested that we cross Meridian Street to buy ice cream cones at Tompkins Ice Cream on the corner. It was a good arrangement for us: we brought back the cones and there was always one for us. In the first summer that Tompkins opened they sold double cones and each side was filled with two dips of ice cream. Four dips for a nickel. What a treat.

It was always exciting when some of the young men gathered in the rear of the court at night armed with flashlights and 22-caliber pistols. We stood in the shadows to watch them flush rats rummaging in the garbage bins behind the Piggly Wiggly grocery store and then shoot them with their pistols.

On winter evenings we gathered around the large floor-model radio to listen to half hours of Amos and Andy, Easy Aces, Eddie Cantor, Fred Allen, Burns and Allen, Edgar Bergen and Charlie McCarthy, Singing Sam the Barbasol Man, and Major Bowes Amateur Hour. Jimmy Fidler gave us the lowdown on the movie stars in Hollywood, and Walter Winchell any gossip he could impart about political figures and New York celebrities.

Jack Benny was one of our favorites, his show opening with a pitch from exuberant Don Wilson about the merits of "J E L L O, Jello in six delicious flavors, strawberry, raspberry, cherry, orange, lemon and lime." Benny worked the same turf year after year playing the miser and taking shots about it from Wilson, Mary Livingston and Rochester, his hoarse-voiced Man Friday. Three lines, a gag and the laugh machine would erupt. Following a formula, the show would break mid-way for a song by one of the resident tenors, Kenny Baker or Dennis Day, and then Wilson would slide into another commerical for Jello, winding up to "look for those big red letters on the box. They spell Jello," and then a group would croon "J E L L Ohhhh."

At 4:30 in the afternoon we'd break from whatever game we were playing to turn on the radio to listen to the adventures of Jack Armstrong, the All-American boy, sponsored by Wheaties, the Breakfast of Champions. Fifteen minutes later we'd resume whatever game we were playing, reassured again that Jack Armstrong had thwarted evil.

Throughout the winter there was usually a board game or a jigsaw puzzle set up on a card table in our living room. Anyone with time to kill would fill in some of the pieces.

May was always special. We kept up on which drivers would

qualify for the 500-Mile Race at the Indianapolis Motor Speedway. On the night before the race and early in the morning on race day we would be out watching the hawkers selling newspapers and cheap souvenirs to the Speedway-bound motorists lined up along 16th Street. We envied the people who bought the souvenirs.

We had a celebrity one step removed in the second grade but we were too young to appreciate it. One of our classmates was the daughter of Louis Schneider, the winner of the race in 1931. That was the year it seemed that half of the cars (each with a riding mechanic) climbed over the wall, the tire from one of the cars killing an eleven-year-old boy playing in his front yard across Georgetown Road.

Had Miss Schneider not left the school we might have used her as the honorary starter for one of the 500-Mile races we staged each year in the rear of Hampton Court. We worked and planned the races for days. We whittled race cars from blocks of pine, affixed roller skate wheels to them on six-inch axles, and pulled them around a dirt track at the rear of the court. We spent hours carefully banking and watering the track. We took on the names of our favorite 500 drivers: Wild Bill Cummings, Kelly Petillo, Wilbur Shaw. One year we had planned to start the race at the same time the 500 was to start—11 am. We were minutes away from the start when Aunt Mary called out the back door for my cousin Jim to come home.

"Time to get these dishes washed," she yelled at him. None of our appeals changed her mind. We ran the race without him. Had Aunt Mary realized how resolute we all were about that race, she would never have deprived Jim of his chance to compete.

That small piece of ground at the rear of the court had many uses; one week a race track, the next week the site of a marbles tourney, another time the site of a track meet. No grass grew there and there was plenty of noise but I can't remember ever being ordered out of the area. The neighbors were a tolerant lot.

The Osbornes were one of the few families in the court who owned a bicycle. The closest most of us got to being mobile was affixing a pair of roller skates to the soles of our shoes. Mothers didn't like them because they often pulled the soles loose from shoes.

Oddly enough, getting new shoes was a treat, but new clothes meant little to the boys, except when they were able to grow out of knickers into long pants. Most of us wore black imitation sheepskin coats each winter, mainly because they were warm and inexpensive. They were good for about one season. By the end of winter we had peeled off most of the coat's shiny, rubber-like coating.

If we sinned at all, it was to sneak a cigarette from some dad's pack or drop water-filled balloons from Baltz's garage roof on the windshield of cars driving down the alley. Generally, the driver slowed down, shouted a curse at us and drove on but on one afternoon, the balloon missed the windshield and went through the driver's window and burst on his lap. He squealed to a stop and dashed out of the car. We all leaped from the roof and scattered through the neighborhood. I hid in a basement window well three blocks away for two hours. One of the group, Charley Crothers, broke his arm when he landed on the ground.

"Where'd they go?" the driver shouted at him.

"That way," Charley responded, gallantly pointing through his pain in the wrong direction.

My First Byline

In the first week of August, 1937, as the summer began to wind down, we looked for ways to occupy our time before school reopened. We had tired of baseball, staged amateur plays, held numerous water fights with garden hoses and had our fill of roller skating. Even the lure of poker in Baltz's basement was gone. We were too old to set up another lemonade stand, so we decided to start a weekly newspaper.

We started with a staff of a dozen, ages ten to thirteen, all residents of the court. By press time of the first issue the staff was down to six. But in the next three weeks we turned out three issues.

It was all so exciting. We had no official editor but each person was assigned duties, some as columnists, some as sports reporters, and some assigned to induce relatives and neighborhood merchants to advertise in the paper. We named it the "Hampton Sentinel." It sold for a nickel a copy.

The lead article in Issue No. 1 was headlined "Freak Accident." It was a three-paragraph story about a man named Elgin Leed, who lived at 2339 North Alabama Street. He was driving east on Ohio Street when a taxicab hit his car from the rear, causing Leed to lose control and strike another cab heading south on Meridian Street. The last line read: "Mr. Leed suffered slight injuries."

That scoop—of absolutely no interest to any of our readers in Hampton Court—came about because I happened to witness the accident. I don't remember how I managed to gather the facts from the policeman at the scene, but I raced home thinking we had authentic news for the first issue.

How proud I was of that byline. I was hooked on the business at the age of twelve with that scoop. Who knows, perhaps that routine traffic accident was why I later spent forty-one years as a newspaperman.

The rest of the paper dealt more with Hampton Court affairs. "Snoops and Scoops" by Salter Finchell disclosed such choice items as:

"Why is it Richard and Edward Drew are so interested in 4310 Broadway? We understand it's because the Welch girls live there."

FLASH! FLASH!

"Jack Leeth has been visiting in the vicinity of Broad Ripple Park a lot lately. We wonder if it is the lure of the water or a certain young lady?"

The Society column, which could have used a copy editor, offered these items:

"Mr. and Mrs. Rucklehouse [sic] entertained her mother and brother from Chevychase [sic], Maryland."

"Julia Sullivan has returned from Peru, Indiana, where she underwent a minor operation."

Page Two featured a piece of fiction by Jean Osborne, age twelve, and three ads; one from the neighorhood movie house "KEEP COOL AT THE CINEMA;" the others came from older brothers, Bill and Nick Connor.

Jean's story was titled The Spanish Seranader. It read:

Rose Marie Gonzalos was sitting alone in the garden thinking of the man of her dreams.

It was about two years ago when Carlos came. He had gone away in the Spanish revolution and Rose Marie had not heard from him since.

Just after the party Rose Marie had come out in the garden to think. Suddenly out of the shadows came a beautiful mellow voice singing their song. She drew back frightened as if to go, but something in the voice seemed only to draw her nearer to the bushes where the voice was hidden.

Upon drawing nearer she discovered it was only her dreams of the man she loved and lost!

Not quite what Cecil B. DeMille was looking for but not bad for a twelve-year-old.

Paul Sullivan's column on hobbies informed his readers:

"Mary Jane Osborne's hobby is eating donuts and toe-dancing."

"Jimmy Connor's hobby is killing ants and riding other people's bicycles."

The first issue was overloaded with items by and about the staff members' families; it didn't sell well. Mother suggested that more residents might buy copies if they or someone living in their apartment got mentioned in the papers, valuable advice for novice journalists.

Soon we found news items about potential customers in most of the twenty-nine apartments.

We improved in looks, if not in content, in the second issue because Dad had the paper mimeographed at his office.

Salter Finchell was back with more gossip; the society column contained ten items and eighteen names. We were learning.

I wrote a five-paragraph short story about some poor soul in Italy in 1890 being tried for a murder he didn't commit. But with some sharp detective work the police learned the real murderer had gone to Spain, so the cops boarded a plane (in 1890?) and found the real criminal and brought him back.

That second issue brought in six ads. Its last page was anchored with a joke making the rounds that read:

"One day a lady by the name of O'Toole asked a lady by the name of Sullivan, "If the Pope should die who would succeed him? "The lady said, 'One of the cardinals.' "

"The other lady said, 'If they do, I hope they don't pick Dizzy Dean.' "

The last issue, dated August 28, 1937, brought in nine ads, including one from the Packard distributor next door to the court, and two used car lots in the neighborhood. The slick issue—renamed "The Court Reporter"—included some droll editors' notes penned by Dad and others who laid out and printed the paper.

"The Court Reporter" ceased publication the week that school resumed.

Printing those papers must have brought back memories for Dad of a similar paper that he had published for his young family some fifteen years earlier. That effort was titled "The Connor Gazette."

There may have been more than one issue but the one still existing was dated January 21, 1921. It was full of hand-printed, droll tidbits about the family: four snapshots of family members pasted on the paper; a few items clipped from the city's newspapers, including an account of his marriage to Mother that was published in June of 1912.

The lead story datelined Taveres, Fla., was an account of Mr. and Mrs. W. D. Seaton (that was Aunt Marie and Uncle Will) arriving from Indianapolis, she with a black eye.

"Some of the guests at the Lakeview wondered about the discolored eye of Mrs. Seaton until she explained it wasn't Mr. Seaton's fault but occurred by her falling on the ice just before starting south on the journey."

Under a headline "Still At Large" was a photograph of a grim Bob Peelle, Mother's brother, holding a shotgun, the caption reading: "Old Man Dynamite the barefoot desperado who is causing the Federal authorities considerable worry is here seen guarding his still in the hills along the banks of Driftwood."

A headline from a newspaper reading "Harding Leaves On Florida Trip" was followed by this news item:

"Mr. Harding would not tell why he is going to Florida but the wise ones and those on the inside know the answer. It is hoped Mr. Seaton will accept Mr. Harding's offer of a place in the Cabinet."

Beneath that story was a caption: "Two good reasons why Mr. Harding is going to Florida." It sat over an ad clipped from a newspaper featuring a shapely pair of female legs encased in black hosiery.

Racy tabloid journalism is nothing new.

Moulded By The Sisters

Most of my memories of the eight years I spent in Cathedral Grade School are murky but not the opening day in Sister Columba's first-grade classroom. It is still vivid sixty-two years later.

Sister Columba was a short, stout woman. Her ample body was encased in the standard garb of the Sisters of Providence: a black floor-length habit with starched white linen breastplate. Her hair was concealed beneath a black and white wimple, a massive rosary hanging from her waist.

She seemed to be cheerful enough when Mother brought me to her classroom on that first day. But in that first hour she called me to the front of the room. And without giving me any reason, she grabbed my head and beat the back of it against the blackboard, giving the rest of the class the first lesson to be learned in her room: behave here or incur my wrath. I never did learn if I had been disciplined for some unknown infraction or whether I was simply the tool she used to set her ground rules.

But I survived that and the next eight years. I was like most of the children in Hampton Court; our lives revolved around that school, and two others, Cathedral High School and St. Agnes Academy—all grouped along 14th Street with the massive SS. Peter & Paul Cathedral, a block south of the court.

The church and school occupied most of our waking moments. There was Mass every morning, at least during the school year. We dressed up for Sunday Mass and Mother sometimes dragged us back in the afternoon for four o'clock vespers service followed by benediction.

Throughout the year we observed holy days and attended novenas and the annual Forty Hours devotions at which the Blessed Sacrament was exposed day and night from Friday morning through Saturday. Each of us were urged to spend an hour praying before the Blessed Sacrament during those forty hours, an hour that never seemed to end. The overnight hours were covered by the men of the parish.

When we reached the eighth grade we attended a retreat, which usually lasted the entire school day. We listened to talks by the priests about such things as sin and redemption and spent time in individual prayer. We were also instructed to maintain strict silence throughout the day, a situation that often produced giggles.

All of these special services were designed to enhance our faith or obtain some special favor, usually for the foreign missions.

The nuns who taught us lived a mostly cloistered life, rarely leaving the school, church or convent grounds. If they did step out, they left in pairs and always dressed in their black robes. They had offered their lives in the service of God and man, and they lived by the three vows of poverty, chastity and obedience. They urged their pupils to follow similar paths in or out of the convent with particular emphasis on obedience.

After Sister Columba's little lesson on the back of my skull, I—and presumably most of the class—learned that first lesson and it carried through the next eight years. I don't remember if I even bothered to report the incident to my parents, knowing even then that to my mother the Church—nuns and priests and brothers—could do no wrong.

How could a mother not think kindly of the nuns when their sons brought home letters like this one that I penned in the first grade and she had saved for nearly a half century:

"I am glad that your feast day comes next Sunday. May is Mary's month. Mary is our heavenly Mother. You are my earthly Mother. God gave you to me. I think He gave me the best Mother in the whole world. I shall always love my two sweet Mothers."

There was a postscript saying "Father Hickey and Sister Columba send their best wishes for God's blessing upon you."

What did it matter that the same letter went to every other mother of a first grader.

Through the next eight grades we were instructed in all of the standard subjects: history, geography, arithmetic, spelling, reading, English and religion. We learned the elegant and graceful Palmer Method in writing, using point-tipped pens that we dipped in ink bottles that sat in holes in the upper corner of the desks. We came home each day with ink stains on the first two fingers of our right hands. Oddly, most of the girls over the years retained the ability to write in that graceful, slanted style; the boys rarely mastered it, or rejected it as feminine.

In the subject of English we spent hours being drilled on parts of speech, subjects, predicates, objects, tense, moods, voice, participles and infinitives and gerunds and sentence diagramming. Who of us mastered restrictive and non-restrictive clauses, subjunctive, indicative and imperative moods? Little wonder that pupils dreaded English composition. Lost somehwere was the romance and excitement of words. We were graded on punctuation and grammar. Content was irrelevant.

Breaks in the daily regimen were rare. No field trips, no in-house movies. We did get called out for fire drills. And once a year we marched out of our rooms and gathered in the hallway to listen to Police Sgt. Magenheimer's annual talk on safety. We were guided to our places in two long rows, kept in line by nuns clicking away with those small toy clickers that you could buy in the dime store.

I left the fourth grade with fond memories of Sister Louise Marie, mainly because she had named me captain of the "Busy Bees," one of the two competing spelling teams. We learned there was only one way to spell: visualize the word, sound it out, memorize and practice. It was Cat—C A T—Cat. Did we actually conquer the rules of spelling—"the final consonant is doubled only when it is preceded by a single vowel in a one-syllable word or in a word of more than one syllable having the accent on the last syllable?" Or did we conquer the subject through practice and memorization? No matter; it has always been a mystery to me why I excelled in that single subject then, and throughout life, while others who later learned the phonics method did so poorly.

The building of character permeated our lives. We were in school to "make something of ourselves." There must be a purpose in everything we did. Sloth was to be avoided because "idle hands are the devil's workshop."

We heard lectures on the Ten Commandments and the Seven Deadly Sins with special emphasis on lust. There was a lot of discussion of heaven and hell, purgatory and limbo, the latter an eternal resting place for babies who died before being baptized. We never got a satisfactory answer to the fate of millions of unbaptized adults in China and India and Africa. Conceivably they could have been saved by having "baptism of desire." But there was no question that we as Catholics had the inside track on getting to heaven provided we adhered to such rules as making our Easter duty (confession and communion at least once a year) and attending Mass on Sunday. Failure to do so meant we had committed a mortal sin and until the sin had been erased by a trip to the confessional we were enroute to a fiery hell.

The trepidation we faced before entering the confessional was only as severe as the sin, but the relief we felt after absolution was almost tangible, a bit like being told by a physician later that a feared "terminal illness" was merely a routine infection.

We believed all of it. It wasn't until well into adulthood that we began questioning the many articles of faith that had been drilled into us. For most adult Catholics it wasn't until Vatican II that we finally were urged to heed our consciences rather than adhering strictly to the rules and regulations that Catholics had been ignoring anyway.

Vatican II was difficult for many who grew up in the thirties and forties. Living your faith was so much simpler when you adhered to rules without question. Many post-fifty-five Catholics would happily return to the twenty-minute Latin Mass. They are still asking if a Saturday wedding Mass "counts" for the Sunday obligation, and feel uncomfortable offering a handshake during the Kiss of Peace in the Mass.

We were living in the twilight of the Victorian Age. Few adults hugged or kissed in public. I sometimes think it was the heavy emphasis on the hazards of sex that made it difficult for so many people to be intimate with the opposite sex. Parents and children seldom mentioned how they loved each other, though it was always implied.

In those grade school days we were warned repeatedly about the evils of materialism, a warning most of us felt comfortable with because we had so little of the world's goods anyway. It was part of the emphasis on building character. The word at school and at home was SACRIFICE.

Boys were the favored sex at Cathedral Grade School. They were the altar boys and the traffic boys. CYO sports were restricted to boys. The girls were allowed to play kickball, but only after the boys had left the playground.

There was little challenge for the girls save the challenge of joining the sisters in a convent. They were taught to be submissive to the male, just as the nuns were subservient to the parish priests. But always be vigilant—and virginal—around the boys. The aim of most girls was marriage by twenty-one, a house full of children at thirty, and security for life. Many followed the dictum only to awaken in their forties, their looks fading, the kids gone, wondering what remained for them besides the Altar Society. It's no wonder that so many welcomed the Pill, despite the Vatican's opposition. It helped to liberate their daughters, giving them limited control over their lives.

The sisters regularly urged the boys and girls to pray for vocations to the religious life. The prayers of three boys and one girl in our class were answered. The boys enrolled in St. Meinrad Seminary in Southern Indiana in the fall of 1939 after graduation from the eighth grade; the girl joined the Benedictine Order at Ferdinand.

The three boys weren't in the group of eighth graders chosen to make the annual spring weekend trip to St. Meinrad by Sister Rose Elvire, who ruled the class. Instead she chose six of us to make the trip, hoping to whet our appetite for the priesthood. None of her selections elected to enroll in the seminary; instead they chose the high school across 14th Street. Maybe Sister Rose Elvire knew the trio was in the bag and she was looking for a bonus or two.

Two of the three boys who enrolled in the fall were ordained; the third left the seminary after a couple of years. Two other classmates later joined the awe-inspiring Trappist Order, but they left, and I long ago lost track of them.

Jack Minta was one of those ordained; the other, Jack Wells, has died. Father Minta is a year away from retirement now, pastor of St. John Church at tiny Osgood, Indiana. He has served as pastor of several parishes in the Indianapolis Archdiocese, including his old Cathedral parish, since his ordination in 1950.

"One summer there were thirty-six guys from Cathedral parish in seminaries," Father Minta recalled. "That must have been in 1940."

Four of the thirty-six came from one family: Joseph, Francis, Paul and James Dooley, the only sons of William J. Dooley, a telegrapher for the old Monon Railroad, and Alice Marie Dooley. The other member of the family, also named Alice Marie, was the lone girl in our class to join an order to become a nun. She left after a couple of years. She never married and spent her life as a teacher at Roncalli High School and in the Indianapolis Public School system before retiring. Two of the brothers, Paul and James, left the priesthood in their forties and married women also in their forties. Neither have children.

It is common for men to leave the priesthood today. It was almost unheard of in the thirties. One who did was the young priest who accompanied us to St. Meinrad that spring of 1939. What a shock it was! I often wondered over the years what the poor man's life must have been like, squeezed by his vows of chastity and obedience on the one side and his desire for love and sex and companionship on the other. Many years later there was talk that he had returned to the priesthood in some distant part of the country.

Although the Ku Klux Klan, which had pretty much ruled the state in the 1920s, had targeted Catholics, even more than Jews and Negroes, we led such sheltered lives that most of the children at Cathedral were unaware of the anti-Catholicism all around us.

The Cathedral parish was booming in those years. The school became so crowded that grades five through eight were taught in a house across the alley from the school. After World War II when the parishioners abandoned the parish in their march to the suburbs, the house had many uses including a CYO club for young single men and women. It wound up as a soup kitchen for the homeless.

Ironically, the grade school building where we were lectured so thoroughly on the hazards of sex has become the Damien Center for victims of AIDS.

A Seventeen-Minute Mass

Living a block from the Cathedral had its drawbacks. It gave the nuns an excuse to frequently assign my cousin Jim and me to serve the 5:30 am Mass.

Barely awake, we stumbled along deserted Meridian Street on cold, dark mornings and then raced into an empty church just in time to throw on our cassocks and surplices and light the candles on the high altar.

Those black, floor-length cassocks, stiff in spots from candle wax, hung inside the tall, wooden wardrobes in the sacristy. The sacristy gave off a dry, musty odor laced with smells of candle wax and wine.

Each morning one of us had to walk to the kitchen in the rectory to fill a cruet with a dry white wine for the Mass. One of those stout, grim women who always seemed to rule such kitchens carefully doled out the wine.

The Cathedral was dedicated in 1906, a structure seemingly built to last for centuries. Its interior was in the Renaissance style, its exterior plain brick except for its classic Roman facade. When the church was renovated in 1936, the temporary wooden front was replaced with limestone Corinthian columns.

The Cathedral was cavernous, seating 1,200. The sanctuary was dominated by a huge, ornate main altar of white marble. It was flanked by generous marble thrones and two marble side altars, one dominated by the Blessed Virgin, the other by St. Joseph. Other equally ornate marble altars sat in niches along the side aisles of the nave. The church looked and felt massive, awesome, quiet.

Huge stained glass windows covered the upper half of the church. The Stations of the Cross lined the lower walls. They depicted in fourteen vivid bas-reliefs the events leading to the Crucifixion and entombment of Jesus. The Roman soldiers looked so fierce as they escorted Christ laboring with his cross on his way to Mount Calvary.

The three 150-foot-long aisles were covered with a thick, hard, rubber-like floor covering adorned with a fleur-de-lis pattern. The church always had a faintly musty smell with a hint of old rubber.

The priests delivered their sermons from the majestic marble pulpit that sat in the church proper. The shell-like roof that hovered over the pulpit was designed to throw the priest's voice to the rear of the church before microphones were used.

The original benefactors would have been appalled when the pulpit, most of the altars, the stations of the cross, the communion railing, and even the pews were stripped from the Cathedral when it was renovated a few years ago.

Michael O'Connor was one of those benefactors. He donated the three main altars when the church opened in 1906. They cost a total of $15,000. The entire Cathedral, including furnishings, cost $180,000.

O'Connor's granddaughter, Betty O'Connor Gillespie, said her grandfather thought the Cathedral should have occupied the entire site without having the rectory attached to it along 14th Street.

"He was so upset with the decision that he wouldn't set foot in the church for ten years," she said.

Ironically, Mrs. Gillespie was a young girl standing in front of the Cathedral in 1936 when President Franklin D. Roosevelt and his procession of cars were held up there briefly on a visit to the city.

"I heard him say, 'They should have built the church on the corner,'" Mrs. Gillespie said, vindicating her grandfather's position thirty years later.

In the 1930s the boys, and sometimes girls, hid in the niches along the north and south walls where the imposing confessional boxes were recessed. You could get lost in the recesses on Sundays when the side aisles were lined with overflow crowds. If there was any horseplay there, it had to be quiet or an usher—or worse still, one of the Sisters of Providence—would rout you out.

At weekday Masses school children left their pews and lined up in those dark recesses to await their turn to enter the confessional, usually with trepidation, depending upon the number and severity of the "impure thoughts" they'd had the week before. Was there any other sin but sex?

In the early years of the decade Bishop Joseph Chartrand often heard confessions. He had a practice of handing out one and five-dollar bills to high school boys after they had confessed. Sally recalled that Bill—otherwise an indifferent Catholic—sometimes went to confession three times a week in hopes he would be on the end of the bishop's largesse.

Our examinations of conscience and penances (usually three Our Fathers, three Hail Marys and an Act of Contrition) got side-tracked some mornings by Froggy O'Toole's clash with the devil. Short, elderly Froggy occupied the same pew each morning near the confessionals on the north side of the church. He usually had the pew to himself. He confessed every morning but not until he had wrestled with the devil, muttering, "Get out, get away from me." As the battle between Froggy and the devil intensified, his voice grew louder and higher.

Froggy was just one of the 4,500 "souls" in the parish in the late 1930s. Fifty years later it was down to less than five-hundred.

One year I was one of two boys selected to carry the bishop's long train at the Christmas Mass. The two of us prepared for that simple task by practicing at home, at church, and at school.

I got an added thrill a few days after Christmas. Our front door bell rang one morning and standing there was Sam (we never knew his last name), dressed in his black suit, a gentle and dignified black man who had been a fixture at the Cathedral for years, an unofficial aide to the bishop, at that time Joseph Elmer Ritter. He opened the church at 5 am each morning and was unobtrusively there until the last communion was distributed at 9 am Children whispered that Sam "talked to the Blessed Virgin" and the nuns did nothing to discourage the talk.

Sam asked to see "Master Lawrence Connor." I was ushered to the door by my mother and Sam handed me an envelope.

"From the bishop," he said simply and left.

Inside was a crisp, new five dollar bill. Or was it ten dollars? No matter; it was a fortune to a ten-year-old boy who could buy an ice cream cone for a nickel. Yet, it was the class with which it was given that stays with me yet.

In those days, especially at the early Masses, the priest breezed through the Mass, rapidly mumbling the Latin which was incompre-

hensible but comforting to the congregation. I can still see Father
Dunn checking his watch as he swept off the altar after a seventeen-
minute Mass to remark, "Let Hickey beat that one."

Father Hickey was one of the half dozen young priests serving
Cathedral parish. He and the others occupied some of the thirty-three
rooms in the rectory, a forbidding mansion of high ceilings, soft foot-
steps and whispers.

As pastor, dour Monsignor Noll ruled the rectory with absolute
authority for twenty-two years. He summoned his charges by stamp-
ing his foot at the base of the ornate staircase and bellowing their
names.

The priests were assigned to officiate at weddings and funerals.
Most of the altar boys serving at weddings were eighth graders because the groom usually gave the altar boys five dollars, and at the
funerals because the nuns wanted experienced servers to avoid any
mishaps.

The funerals were a grim business. Everything seemed to be in
black, including the chasuble (robe) that the priest wore. Any singing by the priest or choir was dolorous. Friends or family members
did not step into the sanctuary to give personal eulogies as they do
today. The priest in his homily tried to reassure the congregation that
the deceased's journey was over and that he or she was enjoying an
eternal reward in Heaven. Sometimes it was hard to picture a hard-
living decedent in the arms of God.

Weddings, then as now, were joyful affairs but they were much
more traditional in the thirties. The bride wore white, the priest wore
white, and the flowers generally were white. Bridesmaids would never
consider wearing anything as startling as the black and white gowns
worn by some attendants today. Nor do I remember the congregation greeting the newlyweds with applause as they waltzed down the
aisle. Clapping in church was unthinkable.

Mass was always celebrated at both funerals and weddings and
both services lasted an hour or more. It was not uncommon for an
altar boy—or even a bride or groom—to topple over in a faint after
kneeling in front of flaming candles for an hour. The flames had a
hypnotic effect.

On Sundays the family attended Mass together. Dad and Mom, Sally, Virginia and I sat together in one pew. Nick, Bill and Bob attended different Masses or sat in different pews if they went with us. We wore our best clothes. Dad always led us into church, setting a good example, though I never felt he was particularly interested in the Mass or the sermons. It distressed me that he never received communion because the nuns contended that Catholics would be barred from heaven if they missed their Easter duty (confession and communion once a year). Somewhere along the way, though, I got reassured that it didn't matter all that much, that there were many routes to heaven.

The Cathedral parish was heavily Irish in the 1930s and 1940s. Over the years the Sons of Erin moved outward and upward as their stations in life improved, their devotion and loyalty to the Church diminishing, their attention given to business and civic endeavors.

Maybe that's what they feared when they warned us in classrooms and churches about the evils of materialism. Still it was those black-robed men and women who had given us the tools to conquer the world: discipline, hard work, a sense that rewards—here or in the hereafter—would be ours if we lived and practiced our religion.

Father George Dunn leads a procession outside the Cathedral in 1939, aided by me as the candle bearer and Robert Emmet Murray as the bearer of the cross.

Virginia in her First Communion dress with her natty brother.

Virginia, Sally and Bo follow orders to look at the camera while posing in front of our rental house at 1731 North Pennsylvania Street in 1931.

Lawrence Connor, a proud new member of the Boy Scouts of America.

THE COURT REPORTER

Third Issue   Price 5 Cents   August 28, 1937

As a "bit of fun", or nonsense, this paper is written by the youngsters of Hampton Court. Average age of the staff members - 12 years. Typed by any-one who will do the work -- who's next?

SNOOPS AND SCOOPS
By Salter Finchell

FLASH!!!   FLASH!!!
Why did Kenneth and "Howdy Folks" Swanson spend their vacations in Princeville, Ill.? Surely not for amorous reasons!

Charley McCarthy lives in the "Lum-ley" - no relative of W.C. Fields' diminutive pal.

Tubby Connor, Jean and Mary Jane Osborne are learning to tap dance. O.K. for the last two - not so sure about Virginia Ann.

"Bo" would like someone to tell him how high is "up".
****

A TRUE AMERICAN BOY
(A Composition)

Many years ago, in the year 1775, during the Revolutionary war, there was a party of young men in the sou-thern part of the Colonies, blocked behind a hill by the English Army, where they were practically helpless.

Finally, the Captain spoke up and said, "We have to get help and plenty of it, but I can't get a man through to General Green." After a bit of silence, one lad by the name of Bob Devore spoke up and said: "Look at that gully over there." The Captain said: "Yes, it goes right through the mountain. The lad said: "How about my going through to reach the General?" "All right, it's a clear path", said the Captain. The lad started with the warning "Be careful of the Red Coats."

In a day he reached the General and started back, but was killed on the way. The American came upon the Red Coats, and gave them a terrific bat-tle, finally outcharging them. The General said the lad he had entrusted with his mission had died as a true American and they should remember him always.
—Larry Connor—   (C.H.S. 1944)—

For one so young, "Bo" goes pretty far back for his characters! (The typist)

SOCIETY
By James Connor -   (C.H.S. 1944)

Miss Nedra Jones is visiting in Rock-port, Indiana.
    * * * *
Threasa Moran is in Batesville for the weekend.
    * * * *
Miss Julia Sullivan is going to Lake Manitou for the weekend.
    * * * *
Miss Marilyn Collins is visiting Leeths in Apt. 5.
    * * * *
Jack Leeth is coming home from Scout Camp Saturday.
    * * * *
Miss Jane Leland is going to enter nursing training at Methodist Hospital next week.
    * * * *
Mrs. Leland is spending a few days in Madison, Indiana.
    * * * *
Betty Lutz and sister had a party for Miss Alice Marie Wooding.
    * * * *
Mrs. T.C. Pilcher and daughter Mary Sue are visiting Mr. and Mrs. Henry Ostrom.
    * * * *
Rosy O'Gorman "pedaled" in from Broad Ripple with Sally C.
    * * * *
Miss Iddy Sullivan is spending two weeks in Wyoming.

Three issues of the Court Reporter were published by the children in Hampton Court during August of 1937.

Unaware that his Dad had died in the stands at Butler Bowl, Bob Connor prepares to throw a forward pass in the game against Washington University of St. Louis.

Bill Connor — center on the Butler University football teams 1936-38.

My Dad, Nicholas J. Connor, sometime in the 1920s.

We're Under Quarantine

Parents feared childhood diseases: diptheria, scarlet fever, small-pox and polio, especially polio. Every school had at least one or two kids with their legs encased in metal braces. People worried a lot about germs. They washed their hands frequently.

In those years before children were inoculated against most of the childhood diseases, families could count on children missing school for two weeks at a time when measles, chicken pox and whooping cough invaded the classrooms. Measles meant bedrest for two weeks in rooms with the blinds drawn to protect the eyes, and an ominous "quarantine" sign went up on the front door.

One winter in the late 1930s I contracted scarlet fever. I knew it must be serious because tall, somber Dr. Courtney showed up at the house dressed in his traditional black suit and carrying his large black bag.

After checking me over he ordered Mother to isolate me in a third-floor bedroom for twenty-one days. He posted a "quarantine" sign on the front door. I was not to leave my bed, despite the fact that I never felt really ill. The only person I saw for those three weeks was Mother bringing me meals, though brothers and sisters occasionally yelled greetings from the doorway or from the second floor. I went to bed with snow on the ground. When I got up on very wobbly legs it was spring. What a marvelous sight it was: the trees had gotten their leaves and the grass was greener than I ever remembered it. The smells of spring engulfed me.

I went back to school but for days I missed my companions: the men and women on the soap operas who paraded their troubled lives on the radio each weekday afternoon. I sat in the classroom wondering how Lorenzo Jones and Helen Trent and throaty Stella Dallas were faring.

Virginia, whose memory—or imagination—is a warehouse of family lore, recalled that Nick grew taller and heavier as a result of the diptheria that put him in bed when he was in grade school.

"It affected his glands," Virginia recalled.

She said he grew so large that in school he needed a desk brought from the high school.

But it was true enough that Nick did tower over the rest of the Connors in pictures taken in the 1920s. He never grew after that and, in fact, seemed to shrink in height and weight as he grew older.

Before the discovery of antibiotics, tuberculosis was another dreaded disease. A cousin, Vincentia Connor Martin, contracted it while serving as a student nurse at St. Vincent's Hospital when it was located on Fall Creek Parkway at Illinois Street. It was the same hospital responsible for her Christian name. She was christened Vincentia because she was the first baby born at the new hospital on February 3, 1913.

As a nurse, Vin was assigned the sole care for a tubercular patient who entered the hospital with a ruptured appendix. Without being given any particular safeguards, Vin spent three months caring for the young woman, she recalled. By the time she was graduated Vin, too, had contracted the disease. Without antibiotics, she spent two years confined to a third-floor bedroom in her Hampton Court apartment. Vin recovered, married, had a family and is alive today.

Our "Colored" Maid

Lou Weaver was one of the thousands of impoverished black women who came north after World War I to work as maids in "white folks" homes.

Each morning on our way to school we'd see them get off the buses and streetcars. Most were stout, middle-aged women, many of them daughters of slaves. They ambled slowly to the houses where they would spend the day washing, ironing, mopping, dusting and sweeping. At five o'clock they would shuffle back to the bus stops carrying battered shopping bags filled with leftover food and castoff clothes. They all seemed to have sore feet.

They traveled home to neighborhoods few of us ever saw. They earned $1.50 a day, plus carfare and lunch.

Lou Weaver began coming to our house in 1927. We loved "Lefty Ludie." Slight, her skin leathery, her disposition gentle under a tough-talking exterior, Ludie worked hard to support her son, Junior, whom I played with on days when she brought him to the house with her. But too often her other son, Ed, who was nearing adulthood when Junior was born, would talk Lou out of her meager earnings with some sad tale. We never saw her husband or husbands, if she had any. We knew almost nothing about her background except that she came north from Tennessee and returned there periodically to visit friends and relatives.

Lou had firm ideas on how children should behave. You did what your parents told you and you didn't argue about it.

Now and then if I misbehaved she would say, "Bozo, you ain't no count." But I knew she didn't mean it.

She made a distinction about blacks.

"There's colored folks and there's niggers," she would expound. Of "troublemakers," she'd say, "them's niggers."

I suppose she would be considered a hopeless Aunt Jemima today. In the thirties she was typical of blacks trying to exist in a white society.

Lou was fond of three items: snuff, pork and bananas.

"I don't smoke, no suh, just lip," she would say.

"Lemme see you spit, Ludie," we'd implore her.

Lou was typical of the few black adults we knew. We saw few of them even though we lived a few short blocks from the principal black ghetto, "the Avenue" which fanned out from Indiana Avenue between 16th Street and the downtown. There were black janitors in some of the apartment buildings and now and then a black man would pull his makeshift cart down an alley calling for "rags and old iron." We rarely saw blacks in the restaurants, grocery and drug stores and movie theaters we visited.

I don't remember ever giving them much thought, though I do remember that most blacks were deferential to whites. Lots of "no suhs, yes suhs" and false laughter. The colored "kept their place" much as they had been taught in the Deep South. Referring to blacks as niggers or coons was common, but for that matter there were lots of references to dagos and wops and kikes, too. We never gave it a thought that we might be racist when we ordered nigger babies at the candy counter, or chanted, "Eenie, meenie, minee, mo, catch a nigger by the toe. If he hollers let him go."

It would be years before blacks themselves forced us to face up to the terrible injustice they endured daily just by being born with black skin.

When the Depression forced Dad to take a deep reduction in his salary, Mother reluctantly told Lou that we would no longer be able to afford for her to work for us. She had been working three days a week.

"Lou said she would work for nothing," Virginia recalled. "She said she'd work for the scraps off the table so she could feed her two kids, so Mom kept her on. She'd give her whatever she had in her pocketbook at the end of the day."

Lou thought her job was in jeopardy one evening when Dad asked her to get him a bottle of spring water. Convinced that the bottled water was healthful for him, he kept a supply in the basement. When she was slow in returning, Dad went to the basement and discovered her filling up one of the empty bottles with tap water from the basement sink. When he learned that Lou had only been following Mother's orders for weeks, Dad laughed about it and told Mother that she could stop buying the bottled water.

Aside from Lou we had little direct contact with black people, or colored, as we referred to Negroes then.

Very few attended grade school with us. Two daughters of the school janitor attended, and I recall one black kid who attended for a brief period in the sixth or seventh grade. It was much the same at Cathedral High School.

Virginia recalled that the Columbia Club would not host the St. Agnes Academy junior prom because two of the girls were black.

One of the few black men we saw regularly was William Able, a gentle giant of a man, who was the caretaker in Hampton Court. He lived alone in a small, hot, musty room by the boiler plant in the rear of the court. William was available day and night to oversee the heating plant, and was on call when any of the tenants had plumbing or electrical problems.

Every morning William would push his large, mobile platform behind each of the back doors and empty the garbage and trash cans. For all I know he burned the residue in the huge furnaces that heated the court. In the summer he mowed the lawns with a push mower and trimmed the hedges that lined the walks. I wondered then if he had a life beyond Hampton Court. If he did, there was no sign of it for he was available at all hours. He had no visitors.

Life was difficult for the Lou Weavers and William Ables. Indianapolis was rigidly segregated. Segregation of blacks in Indiana was mandated by a state law passed in 1869. For fifty years thereafter black children officially had not even been allowed to attend high school. When the Ku Klux Klan ruled the state in the Twenties, Indianapolis opened Crispus Attucks High School in 1927 exclusively for black children. The school remained segregated until 1973. When it opened, the press referred to it as Crispus Attucks Colored High School. It was named after a mulatto who was reported to be the first casualty in the War of Independence.

The Indianapolis City Council even passed an ordinance in 1928 declaring that Negroes could not live north of 30th Street, but it was challenged in court and defeated.

In 1930 about twelve percent of the population in Indianapolis, or less than 40,000, was black. Statewide the percentage was 3.5 percent.

Over the years other maids—black and white—would work for us for awhile and then vanish, but Lou was with us off and on for nearly thirty years. Occasionally, she would board a bus for a lengthy stay with relatives in Tennessee and then she would be back with us. When she was "gettin old and feeble," as she described her condition, she pleaded with Mother to let her live in the basement but it seemed to be out of the question that a white family would have a black person living with them. Instead, Mother and I made the payments on a tiny, two-room house for her in the 2400 block of North Rural Street before I-70 wiped it out a few years after Lou died.

"Here's my shack," she would announce when one of us drove her home. Her "shack" consisted of a kitchen, bathroom, bedroom and living room. The house was wired for electricity.

Mother became furious one day when she showed up at Lou's house and asked if a bathroom she had ordered had been installed. Lou showed her a single spigot sticking out of a wall. Mother had paid the contractor to install a toilet, sink and tub. A member of the City Plan Commission in those days, Mother stormed into City Hall and dragged a reluctant building inspector back to Lou's house to show him what had been done. Lou got her bathroom and the contractor lost his license.

We never knew Lou's age because she never received a birth certificate but she was well into her eighties when she left this world a bent, feeble and bony "darkie," as poor as when she entered it.

Within a week after she died, looters had stripped all of the plumbing appliances from her shack.

Trained By The Brothers

The world beyond Hampton Court began to open when we left the grade school and moved across Meridian Street: the girls to St. Agnes Academy, the boys to Cathedral High School.

At Cathedral the students were Catholics but they came from all sections of the city.

Our lives revolved around books, sports, girls, dances, and trips to the Parkmoor or TeePee drive-ins. Our interests were reflected in "The Memo," the weekly newssheet, and *The Megaphone*, a magazine that came out whenever the copy and editors could get together.

When war came in December, 1941, it seemed remote; fought in places with strange names—Bataan, Corregidor, Monte Cassino, Guadalcanal. It touched us only when we heard that some Cathedral alumnus had been killed, wounded or captured.

Having grown up in the neighborhood, the school yard had been our playground, especially during summers when the Holy Cross brothers had returned to their home base in Notre Dame in South Bend. We were allowed to play in the schoolyard as long as we didn't break a window to bring Mr. Kern, the janitor, from his quarters in the northwest corner of the grounds. We played baseball there, hit tennis balls against the outside wall of the gymnasium or played handball against it. We even tried netless tennis on the rundown tennis court that became the resting place for a surplus airplane Brother Bruno later lodged there, ostensibly as subject matter for his aeronautics course.

We assumed the school had been there forever, though it had been open less than ten years.

In those days Cathedral athletes Johnny Ford and Charlie Shipp and Johnny McMahon had already become legendary figures to us, though they were still in their twenties. We read and reread *Captain Johnny Ford*, the fictionalized account of Cathedral's Jack Armstrong which Brother Ernest wrote about the school's star athlete.

On cold winter nights the family sat in the stands in the gym to watch Bill and Bob play basketball. Afterwards we kids took off our shoes and shot baskets with rolled-up stocking caps.

The gym was very special to us who lived in the Cathedral parish. On some Saturday mornings our grade school basketball team had been allowed to practice there, a treat for boys who usually practiced, if at all, on the outdoor court on the school playground.

We were in the gym on other nights when Cathedral boys teamed with St. Agnes girls to produce operettas. After watching Sigmund Romberg's *The New Moon,* we came out singing "Stout-Hearted Men" while the adults hummed "Lover, Come Back To Me," and "Softly as in a Morning Sunrise." Rita Connor, a cousin, sometimes had a leading role.

If I didn't know the brothers personally, I knew enough about them from Bob and Bill and their friends so they weren't totally strange and forbidding when I entered as a freshman. Those cassock-clad brothers couldn't have been any more fearsome than Sister Rose Elvire, the diminutive disciplinarian who had ruled the seventh and eighth grade boys classes at Cathedral Grade School in a manner that General Patton would have approved.

That first month in high school I was green and apprehensive. We recent Cathedral Grade School graduates stuck close together and were deferential to anyone sophomore or above, and were in awe of upper classmen, especially any noteworthy athletes.

Coming up with the fifty dollars annual tuition fee was a real hardship for many families, including ours, and indeed, some of our friends went to public high schools, mainly Shortridge or Tech, for that reason. Fifty dollars went a long way when gasoline cost seventeen cents a gallon and streetcar fares were seven cents.

In our freshman year we started to realize that there was a world beyond 14th Street. We began to break free of our ghetto mentality, as least free enough to admire the girls at Shortridge, girls we visualized as beautifully tanned blondes wheeling around drive-ins in sleek red convertibles.

When one of our classmates reached the magic age of sixteen and was allowed to drive the family car, the entire city opened up to us.

Ah, the freedom that wheels gave us! A car gave us a chance to visit classmates all over the city. We knew them by their parishes. They didn't live on the North or East or South sides; they lived in

Joan of Arc or Lourdes or St. Catherine. While we weren't conscious of it, those parish designations were offering us a demographic picture of the economic, social and even cultural backgrounds of our friends.

Cathedral was something of a melting pot, attracting boys from all over Indianapolis, but the pot had the aroma of Irish stew. Cathedral had almost no black students, though I remember Otis Bryant, an affable kid who took more punishment from a few teammates in football practice than he ever did in a game. Otis made untiring efforts to be liked and accepted. Could any of us imagine the burdens and frustrations he must have carried? Did we even give it a thought?

In those days, twenty years before Vatican II, we had few doubts about our Catholic faith. We would have expected Cathedral to be staffed by Holy Cross brothers forever.

And what a group they were:

There was Brother Marcian, the stern but fair principal, a strong man seldom seen outside his office that was guarded by the school secretary, Marie Ferris.

I can still see flamboyant Brother Dunston standing on the second-story window sill, threatening to jump because we showed more interest in clowning than in a passage in the New Testament. One of the school's favorites was Brother Pierre. He thought that if we could understand and appreciate and, yes, even memorize Browning's "My Last Duchess" maybe, just maybe, we'd begin to appreciate poetry.

There was Brother Cassian who called upon us as "Mr. A-4" or "Mr. C-5"—our seat designation, never by our names.

Was there ever a teacher more formidable than ponderous Brother Bruno who taught physics and aeronautics? Anyone who sat in front of his desk faced the threat of a heavy paperweight being dropped on his feet should he be foolish enough to prop them against his desk.

"Cotello [sic], upta board," he would bellow at Ed Costello in his guttural accent. I can still see him grabbing my cousin Jim for whistling in the hall, booming out, "What you think you are boy, steam engine?"

Costello and I sometimes relieved the tedium of memorizing

flora and fauna in biology classes by leaving notes or pieces of candy in the recesses of a table that we shared at different class hours. Biology was taught by shy Brother Christian, who chastised errant students by bringing his right hand out of the muff he fashioned from his cassock and dipping a finger at the miscreant.

Typing classes were fun, perhaps because they were an elective. You knew that if you typed a perfect paper you would be commended by gentle Brother Bertin, for "hitting a home run." One of the older brothers, he sported a white goatee. He patrolled the aisles encouraging his charges with little taps on the back.

Did any of us ever conquer Brother Etienne's French classes ("Ooey, ooey, monsur")?

Brother Fidelis tried to jam chemical formulas into thick heads, often shouting, "Tousands and tousands of times I've told you..."

What has happened to those selfless servants in the fifty years that have passed? Did many of them leave the order to join the service during the war? When the Church threw open its windows in Vatican II did the brothers fly out? It never seemed to occur to us that the brothers were religious; that they had joined the Holy Cross order to serve God and man. In the day-to-day effort to force feed education into us, they seemed rather more as forminable adversaries than servants of the Lord.

Did they spend much of their free time in their residential quarters wondering if it was all worthwhile after spending the day dealing with boys more interested in handball than chemistry? In four years at Cathedral I can't recall ever being in the Brothers' quarters. But I got in there on a recent visit. Only now it is part of the Catholic Center that houses the offices of the Indianapolis Archdiocese. Many of the Brothers' bedroom cubicles are counseling rooms for Catholic Charities.

When the school was opened in September 1927, a story in *The Indianapolis Star* reported that the quarters consisted of thirty bedrooms; a chapel, community room, living room, dining room, kitchen and pantry, trunk and laundry rooms, plus a suite of bedrooms and a parlor for a housekeeper and assistants.

On that return tour it was difficult to locate the different classrooms and the study hall because the rooms have been sliced into offices. The ancient band room and cafeteria that sat along 14th Street behind the school were gone; probably leveled when an eight-room annex was added to the school in 1952.

The Indiana Catholic Conference occupies space on the lower level where we had our lockers. Desmond Ryan, who heads the conference, says old grads occasionally pop into his office looking for the spot their lockers occupied. Across the hall are spotless restrooms—a contrast to the old shower rooms that once were there. I half expected to hear lockers banging shut.

Up two flights, walking along the hall's terrazzo floors (now carpeted), I had a similar sensation, expecting the class bell to ring out and see a stampede of boys bursting out of the classrooms.

The gym looks much as it did in those glory days of 1942-43 when the Irish basketball team went 5 and 12, and even parents and girl friends stopped coming to the games by season's end. A reception hall for archdiocesan affairs now, the floor is still lined for basketball but the baskets are gone. So are the bleachers. The stage is hidden by a frayed maroon curtain; the rigging in the ceiling is gone, and the stage is piled high with unused desks and file cabinets.

For my first three years at Cathedral avuncular Joe Harmon was the coach of all three sports: basketball, football and baseball. He probably earned $2,000 or less a year. Joe moved on in my senior year and the school got a new coach. He was Milt Piepul, who tumbled from his pedestal as an All-American fullback at Notre Dame in 1940 and landed at Cathedral as coach of the football and basketball teams after a year playing for the Detroit Lions professional football team. One year at Cathedral was enough for Milt. He moved on to begin a long and successful career at several Eastern colleges as a coach and athletic director. We thought Milt a fearsome figure with his thick glasses and deep throaty voice. An adult figure to us, he couldn't have been half dozen years older than his players.

The outside wall of the gym that served as the handball court now is blocked by a garage. In our class the handball courts were ruled by short, agile guys like Gene Hinderliter, Tony Rene, Mike Raimondi, George Jennings and Ed Roney.

The old schoolyard is now a parking lot. On most mornings the only car parked there in the Forties was a massive LaSalle that brought the McNamara brothers to Cathedral from their farm at Carmel. Almost no students owned cars, and gasoline rationing during the war years kept their parents' cars idle most of the time.

Wandering through those hall, I began to wonder what it was that made Cathedral special; why it was able to turn out so many graduates who later achieved success, despite a curriculum that demanded so little of its charges. A good memory usually meant good grades.

The Brothers must have done something right. Our class of about one hundred produced four physicians, two optometrists and a chiropractor, lawyers and engineers, actors, artists, authors, editors, and a dozen or more graduates who took over family companies. And our class was not much different than other Cathedral classes of that time.

Part of it was the discipline enforced—firm but fair. The principal used the paddle when appropriate. Few parents objected. Part of it, too, was the religious training. We were reminded regularly that our roles in life were to serve God and our fellow men; that we were expected to be honest and fair and work hard. As Catholics, we were expected to set good examples; our faith and education were gifts we dare not squander. The charge we were given at school and at home in those days was SACRIFICE. So it is not surprising that owners of businesses felt safe in choosing such men to run their companies.

In those days Catholics lacked the boldness they display today, one of the effects of the Depression. We were drilled that materialism was evil. Perhaps that's why Cathedral produced so few entrepreneurs. Better to get a steady 8-to-5 job than get out there and chase the almighty dollar.

Or could it have been that our parents inadvertently had passed on the uncertainties that lingered from Ku Klux Klan days that as Catholics we were still outsiders in a Protestant world? We'd better not get too pushy and vocal.

It was a time when girls wore bobby sox over silk hose and saddle shoes. Boys wore corduroy slacks (preferably yellow) and corduroy car coats that hung to mid-thigh. We listened to the big bands of Glenn Miller and the Dorsey brothers on 78 discs and stuffed nick-

els into juke boxes to hear Sinatra sing "I'll Never Smile Again" and
"I'll Be Seeing You." We danced, after a fashion, at the proms at the
Severin Hotel and Westlake to the music of Louie Lowe and the
vocals of Bill Croker.

It was a time to fall in love. Most of the profiles in the weekly
"Memo" newsletter had some reference to the subject's lovelife. Typical was the windup of Ed Galm's profile of Joe Viehmann: "Many
girls occupy his mind, but a cute little northsider, Marjorie Love, is
his favorite."

Every week the "Memo's" Keyhole Kernels carried such teasers
as "Ed Suding knows only one letter of Morse Code—Dot, Dot, Dot."

The Megaphone was highbrow compared to "The Memo." It listed
the Honor Roll, announced upcoming school functions and turned
out students' art works and literary efforts. Tom Nohl enlivened the
pages of the December 1942 issue with a story about death—his own.

Pete Smith outdid Nohl with "Youth Questions His Destiny,"
a three-stanza poem that began:

Into the night's eternal gloom,
I am wandering, always wondering
What the blackness holds in store;
Will it reach forever more
To my heart's abysmal core
And keep it ever pondering?

Pretty heavy thoughts for a guy who spent his adult life in the
entertainment business, first as a Broadway singer and later as a the-
atrical agent.

By the time we were seniors the war had intensified and become
more personal for many of us. Our cousin, Tom Connor, flew his Navy
plane off a carrier in the South Pacific one day and never returned.
It was shot down over Okinawa.

The Allies finally went on the offensive and the songs reflected
it: "I Left My Heart at the Stage Door Canteen." "Coming in on a
Wing and a Prayer," "I Came Here to Talk for Joe." The movie theaters were showing *Mrs. Miniver*, *Casablanca* and *Thirty Seconds Over
Tokyo*.

We began smoking Chesterfields on the sly, and cooly ordering "Calverts and ginger" and "CC and Seven" from bartenders willing to ignore age restrictions.

We spent a lot of our senior year discussing which service we'd join or whether we'd wait for the draft. Some left early to enlist and others got permission to move on to college after the first semester. It was all so exciting and we were anxious to be part of it.

But we soon learned there was a heavy price to pay. Five from our class were killed in action, and two others spent several months in POW camps after being taken prisoner by the Germans. Most of the rest of us spent three long years in places far from home.

Life was never the same for any of us after 1943.

Earning Our Keep

On some Saturday afternoons Dad took Mom to a nearby restaurant for a late lunch, one of the few luxuries my parents allowed themselves.

Before they left, Mom sometimes told Sally and Virginia and me to mop the linoleum floor in the kitchen and pantry. We always groused about the job but sometimes made a game of it, even attracting friends to join us.

At first we made sure the floor was soaked generously with soapy water. Then we lined up near the front door and raced down the hall and slid across the floors. It wasn't the neatest way to mop the floor but it worked. We timed it so that we'd rinse off the floor before Mom and Dad returned.

Mom insisted that we cover the wet linoleum with newspapers to keep dirty feet off the floor until it dried. There weren't any shoe marks on the linoleum but there were plenty of ink marks from the newspapers.

Mopping the kitchen floor was just one of the many household jobs to which the three of us were assigned. After dinner one of us cleared the dining room table, another washed the dishes and another dried them. We dusted and vacuumed at least once a week. It was my job to wash windows in the spring and fall, a job I despised. I never learned how to rid the panes of the streaks that the Bon Ami left on them. It was especially difficult while perched outside on a window sill. One morning I jammed my knee in anger through a large window that refused to open. I expected a tongue lashing from Dad when he got home that evening but he accepted Mother's explanation that it was an accident.

We were never paid for the chores. Weekly allowances were out of the question.

I learned early not to volunteer. I was about nine when I offered to shine my brother Nick's shoes, hoping to please him. He was agreeable and showed me how he wanted them shined.

That evening when he returned home from work he complimented me on the job I had done and gave me a penny. I was pleased.

Two days later he asked if I would like to shine another pair. I agreed, anxious to earn the penny. Soon, though, I learned that a penny didn't buy much.

When summer arrived, he gave me two pairs to shine, one of them two-toned black and white. I diligently cleaned and shined them. It took me most of the morning. I was hoping for a nickel but when he handed me a penny again, I balked. With him looking on, I opened the window in the third-floor bedroom we shared and threw the penny across the court. From then on he shined his own shoes.

I was one of the few boys in the neighborhood who didn't have a paper route but I substituted for a month one summer for Jack Osborne. He had a great route: sixty-five customers in three nearby apartment buildings and ending with a few customers in Hampton Court. It took only about twenty minutes to deliver the route once I figured out how to race through the apartment hallways while sailing papers under the doors.

Collecting was always difficult. The route was supposed to produce four dollars a week profit but I never seemed to end up with much more than two dollars. Trying to collect from the elderly women in those apartments on Friday and Saturday evenings was often futile. I could hear them inside but they knew I was there to collect and they refused to open their doors.

As the month wore on I began to lose money on the route. Two and three times a week a customer would cancel the paper, usually because they left on vacation. I was terrified of the tough-talking station manager and was reluctant to report any stops, and I wasn't picking up any new customers. So throughout the month I continued to draw sixty-five papers each afternoon, even though by the month's end the route had dwindled to thirty-five customers, and I was dumping thirty papers in trash containers.

When Jack came back to take over the route and the station manager learned what I had done, he ordered me never to set foot in the station again. Jack wasn't too happy with me, either.

I feel like some of those old women still owe me.

I got my first real job the summer I turned fourteen. I went to work for Centennial Press, my Uncle Tommy's printing company in the Century Building downtown. I worked a regular forty-hour week. Each Friday afternoon Uncle Tommy handed out small manilla envelopes to his half dozen employees. Mine contained $7. I was thrilled. Seven dollars went a long way when movies cost a dime and milk shakes fifteen cents.

I had a number of tasks—gathering multi-colored forms into stacks before their spines were laced with glue, trimming reams of paper in the huge cutter, running errands, sweeping the floors and cleaning the rollers on the presses with a solvent at the end of the day; a dirty and disagreeable task.

One day Uncle Tommy decided I was ready to feed a thousand postcards into an ancient hand press. He warned me to be careful that I didn't get my hand caught in the press and cautioned me about running the press too rapidly.

"It will take you a long time before you get used to running this press, so take your time," he said.

I was dutiful for the first hour, carefully feeding one card in the press as I pulled the other out. It seemed so routine and boring that I gradually increased the speed of the press and by the end of the day I had the press running at maximum speed. So much for Uncle Tommy's advice.

I worked most summers through high school at Centennial Press.

During the winter I earned four dollars a week as a foul boy at Sturms Bowling Alleys, which had opened in 1938 on Illinois Street behind the court. Two nights a week from six to eleven I sat on a chair in a platform overlooking the alleys watching to see if any of the bowlers stepped over the foul line. When they did I pressed a button that rang a bell and turned on a light at the end of the lane. It's all done automatically now. I got along well with the bowlers because I often day dreamed or dozed and failed to react when they stepped over the foul line. The job paid one dollar per league and I worked two leagues a night. It wasn't much but it was easier and safer than working in the pits setting pins and retrieving the bowling balls like the black guys did.

I didn't realize it at the time, of course, because I was working to earn some spending money, but all of those jobs helped to teach me self-discipline, a quality that served me well throughout my entire life.

Uncle Bob Joins The Family

Not long after Dad died, Mother's brother, Bob Peelle, moved in with us in Hampton Court. Mom's other brother Maurie joined the family six months later. They remained part of the family until their deaths.

It wasn't the first time that we became home to one of Mother's siblings. She had cared for her older sister, Marie Seaton, who was suffering from terminal cancer. That was in the early 1930s when we lived in a house at 1731 North Pennsylvania Street a couple of years before we moved to Hampton Court.

Marie was the eldest of the four Peelle children. (A fifth child, Ruth, lived only nine months after her birth in 1881). Marie was a kind, gentle and playful woman. She and her husband, Will Seaton, occasionally visited us; Uncle Will bringing us a batch of the candy that he produced at home. Uncle Will was a lanky, easygoing sort. I can't recall that he was ever employed. We kids assumed he made a living selling the candy he produced. Aunt Marie worked as a secretary at the Knights of Columbus hall at 13th and Delaware streets. They had no children.

I have only vague memories of Aunt Marie's stay with us. She was confined to a bed in a back bedroom on the second floor. As her pain became more intense, we children rarely went in there. She must have suffered a great deal. On one of the few times Mother complained about our playing in the backyard, she came out distraught one morning and pleaded, "Can't you kids be quiet? Don't you know my sister is upstairs dying."

We didn't grasp the meaning of death, of course, but we did move on to another backyard for the rest of the day.

Virginia remembers the night that Aunt Marie died. It was August 9, 1932. Dad and Mom and she went in the room to say prayers when they heard the death rattle.

The two uncles who moved in with us changed our lives. Uncle Bob became a second father. A dapper gentleman, he had a closetful of expensive suits, silk shirts and colorful ties. He favored two-toned shoes and straw sailor hats in the summer, gray felt fedoras and camel's hair overcoats in the winter. He was rarely without a coat and tie.

He usually took more than an hour to shave, bathe and dress each morning, appearing in the dining room for breakfast about nine am beautifully groomed, his fingernails manicured, smelling of Listerine mouth wash and after-shave cologne. His bald head was always pink and shiny. At five-feet, seven-inches and about 140 pounds, he walked very erect, and at the table his manners were always correct. Uncle Bob radiated gentleness and good will and class.

Mother was always there to serve him a full breakfast of orange juice, bacon and eggs and toast. While enjoying the first of the forty Chesterfield cigarettes he smoked daily, he carefully read *The Indianapolis Star* and especially enjoyed Westbrook Pegler's columns because Pegler wrote scathingly about the Roosevelts: Franklin and Eleanor. Uncle Bob despised Roosevelt and the New Deal, echoing the complaints of aristocratic Easterners and Midwestern conservatives who believed that Roosevelt was a "traitor to his class." He recognized that Pegler's attacks were outrageous but he read his column with glee. If Pegler had a particular biting comment, Uncle Bob would chuckle and remark, "Isn't he awful? I love it."

He usually took a taxi to his downtown office at the accounting firm of Kennedy & Ragan, which later became Ragan, Joyce and Peelle, about 10 am where he would read the *Wall Street Journal* and then spend an hour or so working on some client's books. He left for a leisurely lunch at the Columbia Club, followed by a nap in his office, and then the rest of the afternoon again at his desk. He had clients in several Indiana cities including South Bend, Evansville, Marion and Kokomo which forced him to take periodic bus trips to those cities.

Uncle Bob Peelle was a major influence in our lives. He was a good listener and offered sound advice if asked. The only time I can remember his being personally judgmental was when I returned from three years in the Army Air Corps in the spring of 1946 and told him that I was going to join the "52/20 Club" that summer along with my friends. It was a Federal government program to allow veterans to draw twenty dollars weekly for fifty-two weeks while adjusting to civilian life. Uncle Bob was appalled that I would accept a handout, especially one from the Federal government. So I spent that summer again working at Centennial Press while my ex-army friends lounged around the Riviera Club pool.

Uncle Bob was instrumental in my being admitted to the University of Notre Dame in the fall of 1946. Because returning veterans could finance their college costs through the G. I. Bill, there were far more applicants seeking admission to Notre Dame than the university could accommodate. Uncle Bob was a business friend of P. C. Reilly, an Indianapolis industrialist who was a major benefactor of the university. A word from Mr. Reilly was all that was needed for me to gain acceptance.

At that time I was still pondering my future. I had considered studying engineering because engineers seemed to be in demand and were well paid, but dropped the idea after realizing I had taken basic Algebra four different times and never gotten a grade above seventy-one. Hotel and restaurant management was a new academic field that was being touted as lucrative and exciting. Forget it, Uncle Bob cautioned me.

"You can't believe the headaches of running a hotel," he cautioned. "I've been around a lot of hotel managers who complained about the problems they face every day—drunks, thieves, people who don't pay their bills, people who tear up the places. Not an easy job."

What kind of a job did I want? he asked. I told him that I had always wanted to become a newspaperman but realized the pay in those days was poor.

"Do it," he said. "The money will come."

Then he confessed that he had been an accountant his entire life and had "hated every minute of it."

"Do something you'll enjoy," he said.

It was the best advice I ever received.

Being an accountant in a firm in which he was a partner may not have been very exciting but it kept him dressed impeccably, and allowed him to join the exclusive Columbia Club favored by wealthy Republicans, drink Johnnie Walker Scotch whiskey (sometimes with milk when his ulcer was active), and eat at fine restaurants. He was quick to pick up the drink and dinner tabs, as well.

Uncle Bob had a brief, happy marriage to a woman we all loved.

Her name was Florence Bird. She was divorced with two children. Uncle Bob had dated her for several years but they had not married because of her divorce. However, when her son, Dick, twelve, was killed by a car while riding his bicycle, Florence fell into a deep depression. Uncle Bob decided to go ahead with the marriage in an effort to bring her out of the depression.

Their marriage was brief but idyllic. It was marred for a time only because he had married a divorced woman, thus excluding him from his Catholic faith. It bothered him and it bothered Mother, but it was resolved when a priest decided that because Florence had never been baptized they were free to remarry in the Church. Both were in their forties when they married and they produced no children.

A pre-schooler when they married, I have almost no recollection of what Aunt Florence looked like, though I'm told she was short, somewhat chunky with a pretty face and tiny feet. I do have a warm feeling about her after sixty years. She died of leukemia less than two years after they married. Uncle Bob was devastated. He moved to the Barton House, a second-rate residential hotel in downtown Indianapolis that later was turned into a nursing home. He became somewhat reclusive for the next ten years or more. I'm sure Mother induced him to live with us after Dad died just so she could get him out of the place. And he, in turn, realized that Mother would need financial assistance to house and feed her family after Dad died. Their joint decision was a fortunate one for all of us.

Uncle Bob lived with us in Hampton Court until he died at the age of seventy. In the last few months of his life, he spent less and less time with the family; often retiring to his room after supper to say a rosary. While we knew he had suffered from an ulcer and diabetes for ten years or more, we did not learn of the cancer that was attacking his stomach until he entered St. Vincent Hospital for an operation to remove the tumor. The cancer proved to be inoperable and he died on October 11, 1952 of a heart attack the day after surgery.

We had assumed from his generosity and his prosperous lifestyle that he was well off financially, but a few weeks after his death we learned that he left no fortune. In fact, he had borrowed heavily on his insurance policies. He left this world with a closetful of high-priced suits and a few unpaid bills.

The Connor Cocktail Party

Throughout the 1950s we hosted an annual Christmas holiday cocktail party. Each of us invited our friends. Bill, who rarely drank more than a bottle of beer a week, generously bought the spirits.

When the party got rolling around 6 o'clock well over 100 guests would be jammed into the house at 3901 Park Avenue where we moved after leaving Hampton Court in 1952. Despite one of her standard aphorisms—"You don't have to drink to have a good time"—Mother was tolerant of the drinking because she loved visiting with the guests. The party was popular because it turned into an annual reunion of old friends.

That first year we learned a lot about hosting a cocktail party. We had hired a young black man as bartender. A co-worker of Uncle Maurie's, Eddie had tended bar at other parties, Maurie insisted. So it was a surprise when we spotted Eddie studying a bartender's manual when the first guest asked for a martini.

When we realized that it would be difficult to serve an overflow crowd from a makeshift bar in the kitchen, we decided to mix large batches of martinis and manhattans and circulate through the rooms, refilling glasses with the lethal spirits. By 7 pm a steady procession of guests were walking around the block, trying to clear their heads.

When the party wound down, Eddie had begun to show the effects of his own imbibing, circulating through the crowd shaking hands and making small talk. It was Eddie's only appearance. In subsequent parties, family members manned the bar. Guests were served a manhattan or a martini upon request. The rest got highballs with generous amounts of mix.

As the evening wore on at the first party, Uncle Maurie became a conspicuous presence, so Bill and Mom insisted that he stay in his second-floor bedroom during subsequent parties. It had little effect, though. Maurie had something witty to say to guests lined up to use the bathroom. By the time they headed downstairs, he had induced them to bring him a drink on their next trip upstairs.

Everyone liked Uncle Maurie. Such a witty fellow.

♣   ♣

Mom Bears Her Cross

Mother had her crosses to bear in a long life but none was heavier than her brother Maurie.

He came to live with us in 1940 and he stayed on until death took him thirty-four years later. Uncle Maurie moved in with us about six months after his brother Bob joined the family.

Uncle Maurie was broke when he arrived and he was broke when he died at the age of eighty-nine. He lived and died broke because he worked sporadically. And when he did work, he spent his pay-checks on whatever spirits were available, though cheap wine and beer were his spirits of choice.

Why Aunt Lois divorced him in the mid-thirties never was dis-cussed in front of us children, but we surmised that she had had enough of his drinking and his unreliability. She was raising their two daughters, Judy and Margaret, and didn't need to raise a middle-aged child as well.

Sensing that Maurie adrift was headed for life as a homeless wino, Mother and Uncle Bob brought him into the family. He enlivened life for all of us.

Maurie's fondness for beer and wine was his shield and his sister's cross. Mother, a teetotaler, simply could not understand why Maurie imbided whenever he got the opportunity.

Fortified with cheap wine, Maurie became arrogant, sarcastic, and iconclastic, usually aiming his barbs at the Catholic Church, though he liked to give the impression he had his own links with the Almighty. He had a droll and sometimes biting wit which outsiders found amusing.

Mother never could come to terms with Maurie's drinking. When he drank he created tension in the family, mainly because he angered Mother.

After she had lectured him, he would retort, "All right, Mrs. Jesus," or "It's hell living with a saint." He spent most of the last third of his life with Mother and Bill because the rest of us had married and left home. When he showed signs of drinking, Bill would scour the house seeking the bottle of wine he had secreted. When located, it went down the toilet, a terrible waste in Maurie's estimation.

When not drinking, he was quiet and even reserved. Where his brother Bob was dapper and socially correct, Maurie wore a suit and tie (always a bow tie) only to weddings and wakes; the rest of the time he wore unattractive, and usually secondhand, sportshirts for days at a time. He didn't bother to shave daily, and he rarely visited the barbershop.

He spent his days devouring the three or four books (mostly nonfiction) he brought home each week from the neighborhood library. He once told me that he had read Emil Ludwig's *The Nile* at least twelve times. He rarely discussed the books he had read or what ideas they generated in him. Maurie was very intelligent but I think he read all those books as one more shield against a life he didn't enjoy. Or it may have been simply a way to deal with boredom.

The closest he ever came to divulging his inner thoughts were in amateurish poems he sometimes wrote when he was drinking; the poems usually profane or iconoclastic. In one he titled "Missionaries' Dilemma," he wrote:

Renounce your foolish idols
Your vicious demon's ire
Meet the one true god
Our loving sire,
Who roasts his children
In eternal fire.

I can't remember his ever talking about Aunt Lois or his daughters who had married and long since moved to other cities. The daughters didn't contact him, though I vaguely recall Judy once making a passing effort at reconciliation. It was not Maurie's nature to show sentiment of any kind.

His standard reply to anyone asking "How are you?" was always, "Still breathing."

It was as though Maurie didn't want to cope with life so he remained something of a child, though not childlike. His refusal to deal with life may have begun with the death of his father when Maurie was nine years old.

His wit was evident even as a child. In an effort to teach her children etiquette, Grandma Peelle one afternoon instructed Maurie and his sister Marie the proper way to greet guests at the front door. On this afternoon she was expecting several neighbor women for afternoon tea. Marie, who was thirteen, was assigned the role of visitor; Maurie, eight, was to greet her.

Marie went to the front door, twirled the doorbell and Maurie answered the ring.

"Good afternoon Maurice," Marie said. "Is your mother at home?"

"Why yes she is Miss Peelle," he answered. "Won't you come in?"

He then escorted her across the parlor to a chair. "Please have a seat," he said. "I'll tell Mother that you are here."

But as she seated herself, Marie broke wind audibly.

Maurie turned and said, "Make yourself at home. Poop if you want to."

Both he and his brother Bob attended boarding school at what is now St. Joseph College at Rensselaer in northwestern Indiana in the mid-1890s because their widowed mother was unable to raise four young children alone at that time. Maurie recounted in later years that Indians were still living in tepees in the area when they were in school.

He liked to tell the story of Old Tom at St. Joe.

One Sunday morning, he said, they found Old Tom dead in his stall. Tom was an aged horse which had pulled the milk truck around the campus in the early morning for nearly fifteen years. Most of the boys were saddened at Tom's death but by noontime they had momentarily forgotten it. They had their minds on the weekly feast, the Sunday dinner. After they had said grace and their plates were full, they were given the signal to begin eating. At that moment one of the boys bellowed, "Whoa Tom!" A silence settled over the mess hall. Then each boy placed his fork on the table and quietly left the room.

Though he abhorred exercise in his later years, Uncle Maurie had been an outstanding athlete in his youth. Short like his brother Bob, Maurie had been a par-shooting golfer, a semi-professional baseball player, and a member, along with Bob, of a professional roller polo team. Similar to ice hockey but played indoors on roller skates on a wooden floor forty by eighty feet, roller polo was very popular at the turn of the century. (A similar sport called Roller-Blading or Roller Hockey, in which the players skate on in-line skates, has become popular today.) The skates and the body checking against the boards created deafening noise, and the action was fast and dangerous. The players carried four-foot long sticks like those used in field hockey. The aim was to drive a red, hard rubber ball past a well-protected goalie into a net. Their team played in the Cyclorama Rink, which later became the site of the Traction Terminal on West Market Street a block from Monument Circle.

He often recounted how as a young man he accompanied Carl Fisher, the man who helped to build the Indianapolis Motor Speedway and later created Miami Beach, on a cross-country automobile race over dirt roads and trails through Atlanta and eventually reaching Miami. It may have followed the route of the Dixie Highway that linked the north to Florida.

As a young man he was induced to accept a blind date with the daughter of Stoughton Fletcher Jr., the millionaire banker who lived in Laurel Hall, a two-million-dollar mansion that over the years became the home of Ladywood School and currently is home to the Hudson Institute think tank. Maurie arrived at the mansion with his friend. They waited several minutes in the foyer for the young woman. About the time they decided to give up and leave, the woman slowly descended the grand staircase. But she was in no shape to leave the house. She was naked.

Maurie was always a bit jealous of Mother. After she was appointed to the city's board of park commissioners, she came home from her first meeting and found all four burners on the stove boiling large pots of potatoes.

"What the hell are you doing, Maurie?" she asked.

"Well, I thought since you had been named to the park board I thought you might be bringing home some of your political friends for supper," he replied. She knew automatically that he had been drinking.

Part of his jealousy was due to Mom's success in politics. Maurie had worked in the county assessor's office for several years but had never held any important posts.

Maurie created many embarrassing and trying moments whenever he found enough cash to buy wine.

Uncle Bob recalled one early evening when he had boarded a bus home and it was stalled at Ohio and Pennsylvania streets for several minutes.

"What's the problem?" Bob asked the bus driver.

"Ah, some damned drunk is out there directing traffic," he said.

Bob looked out the window and saw that it was Maurie. He said he ducked so Maurie wouldn't see him.

One evening during the war, Maurie announced that he was heading for the drug store, so Mom asked him to pick up some V-mail paper so that she could send letters overseas to servicemen. He made her repeat the request.

He returned with a box of Kotex.

"What the hell is that?" she yelled at him.

"Well, you said female paper, didn't you?" he retorted.

He left the house one morning dressed in a white linen suit, probably one he had inherited from his brother Bob. He returned three mornings later. Uncle Bob was standing at the front window in Hampton Court waiting for a taxi when he spied Maurie staggering up the walk. When Maurie lost his balance and fell into the hedge, Bob hollered to Mother in the kitchen, "Hey Ag, come here and look at this goddamned grasshopper."

When Maurie finally stumbled into the house, Mother began berating him. Assuming a regal pose, Maurie slowly raised his palm and said: "Ag, has the dry cleaners returned my coronation robe?"

Usually such incidents ended with Mom shaking her fist at Maurie and jumping up and down in anger; her face crimson. Maurie would then slink off to his room and stay out of sight until the following morning.

On another afternoon Mother became alarmed when she learned that Maurie was standing on the corner passing out dimes to the children coming home from St. Joan of Arc School. His intentions might have been noble, but he could easily have ended up in jail as a child molester, she feared.

In Maurie's twilight years Bill had an agreement with Maurie that allowed him to purchase a six-pack of beer when he received his Social Security check each month; the rest of the check went to

Mother, ostensibly for household expenses, but mainly to keep Maurie from using it to purchase cheap wine.

As he grew older Maurie became forgetful; sometimes dropping cigarette ashes into trays that Mother had filled with hard candy for her grandchildren. It never deterred them from eating the candy.

When his great niece, Tina Connor, once asked him why he thought he had lived so long, he told her he once was shocked by a high power line; that he jumped twenty feet in the air and every germ in his body had been been cleansed from him. On another occasion he answered the same question by telling Tina to look outdoors at the shrubbery. He never explained.

Maurie had a rugged constitution. He lived eighty-nine years despite smoking two packs of cigarettes a day, drinking whatever alcohol he could find, eschewing exercise, and eating very little food. In fact, his favorite breakfast was a raw egg in a glass of beer.

Maurie's brand of cigarettes was Raleigh, principally because each pack carried a coupon. When Maurie amassed hundreds of the coupons he would redeem them for goods, usually a small appliance such as a toaster or a mixer. He seemed to glow when he presented them to Mother as a gift.

Perhaps sensing that her death was imminent, Aunt Lois called Mother to ask if she would relay to Maurie that she was sorry about her lack of tolerance and about the divorce. Mother carried out her wishes but after Aunt Lois died Mother insisted that Maurie not attend the funeral, fearing that his appearance would upset his two daughters who had been estranged from him since the divorce.

Maurie died in the same nursing home where Mother spent her last months. Unhappy there, he refused to eat and lasted only two weeks.

I happened to be there when he died. As I entered his room, two nurse's aides were screaming hysterically. They had just come across him lying unconscious on the floor. I called for a registered nurse who checked his pulse and asked me:

"How far do you want to go to save him? We can send him across the street (86th) to St. Vincent's."

"Let him go," I said. Death came within an hour.

He had been wanting to die for several years.

The Opposite Sex

By the time the 1940s rolled around, our interests had switched from kick-the-can and penny-ante poker to the opposite sex.

We had played postoffice and spin the milk bottle at boy-girl birthday parties in the seventh and eighth grades, though we never let the nuns know about them. While being closeted with a girl was exciting, it was no real sexual encounter. Most of the time we spent the minutes in the closet giggling until time was up. Few of us actually kissed.

We had been repeatedly cautioned about the hazards of sex by the sisters from the time they separated us into single-sex classrooms in the fifth grade. Impure thoughts were to be rigorously avoided. We were told that sex was for procreating. Period.

Any boy who masturbated ran the risk of going to hell and arriving there blind. The sisters avoided the term; instead they employed a biblical phrase, "dropping your seed." Being slow in such matters, I had this vision of boys scattering vegetable seeds along a roadway somewhere.

How ignorant and naive we all were. Even as freshmen in high school we believed outlandish tales about sex, including a report that one of our more adventurous classmates from grade school had been having sex so often that his penis had worn down to a nub. But what could you expect; he was attending Shortridge High School.

When we got to high school, it was exciting just to walk or drive slowly past a building at 29 West 9th Street, reportedly a house of ill repute. Some of the bolder boys watched the girls undress in the Bertha Ballard Home from the windows of the Roberts Park Methodist Church next door until the minister caught them at it one afternoon.

Still it was a safer world then. I can't recall any girl in high school getting pregnant. Abortion was an unthinkable option. It was decades before AIDS showed up. Divorce was considered tragic, if not scandalous.

In that environment, we thought the annual New Years Eve parties at the Osbornes an exciting night. The first one was held in

1938, the year I was in the eighth grade. Clarence and Florence Osborne, parents of the three Osborne children, and all of the roomers in Apartment 1 were out attending grownup parties so the kids gathered at the Osbornes to drink cokes, eat snacks, dance, and play ping pong. Each year the party grew. Jean Osborne Gill recalled:

"We danced, ate, kissed the New Year in and went to 5 am Mass at Cathedral on January 1. No one ever complained and the party never caused a problem. We loved it. I can't imagine a party like that now."

It wasn't always so innocent. As the years went by some of the older boys slipped out to spike their drinks from half pints of Calverts or 7-Crown. On the morning after one party, the Osborne family was having a late breakfast at their dining room table when one of the partygoers surprised the family by popping up from behind the couch in the living room and lurching out the front door. That may have signaled that there were to be no more New Years Eve parties in Apartment 1.

I double-dated with my cousin Jim on our first dance. We were freshmen and it took a lot of nerve to ask the girls, even though I asked Jean Osborne, a playmate for five years. Jim asked an Eastside girl, Mary Ellen Quill.

We had no way of getting to the dance at Westlake, a popular dance hall on the far Westside, so Nick agreed to drive us. His sweetheart, Mary Harrison, later his wife, rode along and they arranged to pick us up when the dance ended at eleven o'clock.

Jim and I got the obligatory first dance out of the way and spent the rest of the evening safely huddled with other freshmen boys while the girls gathered at the tables, occasionally pairing off to dance with each other.

After the dance ended, Jim and I wanted to follow the script that called for stopping for a hamburger and a coke at a drive-in. Nick balked because he said he had to get up early to go to work in the morning, but Mary brought him around. Nick finally obliged in good humor but he bawled me out after we got home because I had walked away with Jim when we reached Hampton Court, leaving Nick to escort Jean to her front door.

Groping through puberty, we reached the stage where a major thrill was having your date slide across the seat of the car to sit next to you. I spent hours considering how I could get my arm around some girl without being rejected.

A baby-faced Frank Sinatra had the girls—and boys, too— mooning over his ballads, "There Are Such Things" and "I'll Be Seeing You."

Most of us never did achieve much self esteem with the girls in high school. We had been so indoctrinated about the pitfalls and evils of sex that it was the fear of mortal sin, rather than the fear of pregnancy, that kept us all so chaste. I don't recall much talk about anyone having sex in high school. Going steady was as advanced as we got.

It was enough to be in love. There was nothing quite like that first real romance. Fifty years later a warm spring day, an old song or the scent of a gardenia can bring it all back for an instant and then it's gone.

It seemed like she was in my thoughts every hour I was awake. What was she doing at that moment? When would I next see her? Was she dating anyone else? What was she wearing? I always seemed to see her in a form-fitting fire-engine red suit she wore during the Christmas season. I couldn't concentrate on my studies at school and at home.

We talked on the phone for hours at night, though I can't recall a single subject we discussed. Even a drive by her house was exciting, wondering if she was inside.

Nothing was quite so thrilling as holding hands. I remember that first kiss, so quick and so clumsy, in the living room of her home. The humiliation lasted for days.

It says something about emotions that a half century later the sensations of that first romance can still be so vivid but the object of it all has faded, her face not even a dim memory.

Perhaps it's just as well. The romance was over in six months. She dumped me for my best friend.

A Family of Athletes

I was excited that Saturday morning in September 1935 when our Cathedral Grade School football coach, short on bodies, named me, a fifth grader, to start at end in the opening game of the CYO fifth-sixth grade football season. I had often fantasized while walking proudly to practice in my cleated shoes and oversized uniform that I would catch a game-winning touchdown pass (one-handed, of course) in the end zone at one of the games.

I weighed no more than sixty-five pounds when I lined up with the rest of the team to receive the kickoff. We were playing against Holy Trinity, a school in a rugged Slovakian neighborhood on the West Side. I was surprised—and alarmed—to see the ball bounce toward me, so I hesitated, hoping some halfback would come by and pick it up. It was up to me so I tucked the ball under my arm and started up field when two rugged little linemen hit me from two sides.

When I got to my feet my head was spinning. At that instant I knew football was not my game, though I continued playing for the next four years. But I was always careful to avoid direct contact and managed to give the impression that I was involved by piling on after one of my teammates had made a tackle. I made sure, though, that when I got home to face my brothers I was wearing a grass-stained uniform.

I was placed in this uncomfortable and devious position because of family tradition, but I really wasn't fooling anyone.

There was no question about my playing football. All three of my brothers had been outstanding players; Bill and Bob both on winning high school teams at Cathedral and again at Butler, and Nick had been starting guard on Cathedral's state championship team of 1931, followed by two years on the reserve team at Notre Dame.

Sports of all kind were the Connors common interest, parents included.

Before he was married Dad played basketball on the Young Men's Institute team. He's in one of those old team photos where the players are lined up sidewise; their bearings erect, shoulders back, serious faces looking at the camera. A slim and handsome young man, he looked to weigh no more than 130 pounds.

Even after he developed an oversized waist, Dad still enjoyed bowling, golf, and his weekly workout of handball at the Hoosier Athletic Club.

Mother, too, was athletic. She was something of a tomboy as a girl, throwing a ball like a boy and playing serious tennis, often against males. She and her friends played tennis in long dresses and petticoats on sand-covered courts. This was at the turn of the century.

In an interview with Mary Ann Butters, a reporter for *The Star*, when she was seventy-nine, Mom recalled that hot weather didn't stop them from playing.

"I used to shock Mother when it was one-hundred degrees and I'd run and grab my racket and go on out to play," she said. "Of course, it was hot with the petticoats and all the junk we wore."

If it wasn't football, the Connors were playing basketball, baseball, softball, golf, tennis, bowling, boxing, wrestling, and ping pong when weather kept them indoors. None of us were swimmers because there were no swimming pools or public parks within miles of our neighborhood. Our urban environment ruled out camping, hunting and fishing.

One of the few games Bill missed in high school was a basketball game against Martinsville. On the afternoon of the game he and Bob Shields, a team member and a Hampton Court neighbor, were caught sneaking into the Lyric Theater and were taken by the police to the city lockup. Uncle Harry, a detective on the force, interceded and got them released. The episode seemed humorous to him but he never indicated that to the boys.

At Dad's secret request, the coach, Joe Dienhart, benched the pair in the game that night. Ironically, Bob played one of the best games of his high school career that night. He, too, had slipped into the theater but was not caught.

Virginia and Sally had no opportunity to compete in sports, but they were loyal fans, and they married athletes: Virginia to John Grande, captain of his 1943 Cathedral football team, and Sally to Bill Lynch, an outstanding golfer. Their son Bill became the family's most illustrious athlete. His prowess in three sports at Chatard High School earned him *The Indianapolis Star's* "Athlete of the Year" award, and at Butler he became the school's all-time passing leader as a quarterback.

Bill Lynch was not the only second-generation athlete. Bob's son Robert Peelle Connor was an outstanding two-sport athlete at Chatard High School and Butler; Virginia's son wrestled at Cathedral High School and St. Joseph's College at Rensselaer, Indiana. Nick's son, Steve, was an outstanding football and baseball player at Brebeuf Preparatory School in Indianapolis. Our son Mike was a starter four years on the basketball team at DePauw and was the school's fifth leading scorer when he graduated in 1988. And his sister, Julie, was a starter on the Chatard volleyball team which went to the state finals when she was a senior.

My football career should have ended in grade school but I gave it another try in my junior year in high school. I finally got to dress for the final varsity game of the season. We were playing Washington High School. Thirty players dressed for the game, but we had only twenty-nine matching uniforms so I was given a different colored jersey. I didn't mind. I only hoped that I would play in my first varsity game.

Three quarters went by and I hadn't gotten the call. But late in the fourth quarter Coach Joe Harmon sent me in.

At that time, we had a set play that if the ball was downed on one side of the field, the end on the opposite side was to sneak out near the sidelines as a sleeper so he could catch a pass unmolested.

I was the sleeper. At first the Washington crowd yelled "sleeper" but then they lost interest. After all their team was ahead 39 to 0. Perhaps it was because I had a different colored jersey, but none of the Washington secondary even bothered to cover me.

Marooned on the sideline for three running plays, I began to get embarrassed, so I raced back to the huddle.

"Where'd you come from, Bo?" the quarterback, Jim Dilger, asked.

"I've been out there as a sleeper for three plays," I shouted. "I've been wide open. Why didn't you throw me the ball?"

"Sorry Bo," he said. "I didn't see you."

At that the gun sounded ending the game.

So much for my football career.

So I concentrated on basketball. In my senior year I had been elected captain by the seniors on the previous year's team. We had a new coach, Milt Piepul, an All-American fullback at Notre Dame who was hired to coach both football and basketball. He knew little more about basketball than his charges and we compiled a dismal 5-12 record.

Basketball that year provided two other humiliating moments that remain vivid a half century later.

We played the preliminary to a Butler game at the cavernous fieldhouse. We looked forward to playing there for days. As captain, I led the team out on the floor. I threw up the first practice shot. The size of the fieldhouse must have overwhelmed me because the ball sailed over the backboard and landed in the stands. At that early hour, there were no fans in the seats to retrieve the ball, so I had to climb up into the stands to get it.

I had an opportunity to redeem myself and go out as a winner in the last game of the season. We were playing St. Mary's of Anderson on their floor. We were behind 29 to 30 and I was fouled just as the final gun sounded. I had a chance to tie the game and put it into overtime. I felt confident. Up until then I had been hitting sixty-seven percent of my free throws.

After a timeout that seemed to last until midnight, I stepped up to the foul line, bounced the ball a couple of times, took careful aim and tossed the ball underhanded toward the basket.

It fell two feet short.

My Brother Bill

It was a cold winter night in the late 1930s. My brother Bill and some of his friends at Butler were selling soft drinks, popcorn and apples at the Tuesday night wrestling matches in the Indiana National Guard Armory in downtown Indianapolis to earn a couple of dollars.

Peddling apples that night, Bill sent one down a row to a fan and waited for the return payment, but the fan simply ignored him, grinning at his buddies.

Bill made no fuss. He simply noted the man's seat location, walked down the steps and headed under the stands. After he made sure of his prey, Bill reached up and yanked one shoe from the man's foot and threw it out of sight. He calmly walked back to selling apples.

You didn't short Bill Connor.

Of all of the Connors Bill most resembled Dad both in looks and in personality: short, strong, handsome with dark hair. Both adhered to rigid standards of conduct; life for them was black or white, rarely gray.

I thought Bill the most interesting member of the family, certainly not always the most lovable because he could be short-tempered, intolerant, racist, sexist and opinionated. But he could also be generous and thoughtful, and loyal, too, if he thought the person merited his loyalty. His droll sense of humor softened some of his more caustic traits.

A loner and bachelor, he never fully embraced life. He rarely ventured off the island he built for himself as a young man. After he graduated from Butler University, I can't recall that he ever joined any organization except Butler's monogram club of former athletes. Nor did he volunteer in any civic or religious endeavors, though he may have supported some with money. In fact, he tended to think that the poor were poor mostly through their own fault. He never quite understood that he was one of the world's fortunate few, a white American male with good health, good looks, brains, talent and opportunities.

Bill was a lifelong competitor and his opponent over time became Bill Connor himself. As a boy he often arrived home with torn and bloody clothes but never vanquished, never subdued.

In many respects Bill was the quintessential Virgo: neat, clean, tidy, organized; each tool, each sock in its proper place.

His two-room basement workshop was stocked with the finest tools. There were few woodworking jobs he couldn't perform. The workshop was filled with shiny power tools and cabinets carefully filled, and carefully tagged, with all sizes of nuts, bolts, nails, screws. The walls always seemed to be freshly painted and no paint stains marred the smooth and shiny gray floors. Whatever sawdust accumulated was gone before the lights were turned off at the end of the day. Bill was meticulous, refusing to release a work that was not done to his exact standards. Shortly after I married, he constructed a coffee table fashioned from a long cut of Australian red gum, an extremely heavy, hard wood. Bill worked off and on for nearly a year transforming it into a six-foot coffee table that weighs in excess of 300 pounds. He painstakingly filled the checks and holes in the board and sanded it repeatedly. After thirty-five years the table still has its original finish. It's the one piece of furniture that each of our children has announced he or she would like to own.

While not particularly creative, Bill was an excellent craftsman. I still have the bust he carved of me when I was fifteen years old. He fashioned it from photographs he took of me from all sides.

Thirty years later he took up the hobby again, carving large blocks of pine into busts of Presidents Lincoln and Kennedy. He spent two weeks carving the first bust of Lincoln. Not satisfied, he came up with a second version two months later. Still not satisfied, he spent three months on a third bust of Abe, one finally he thought acceptable.

Bill spent hours in the evening, carving while watching sporting events or old John Wayne movies. He enjoyed history, particularly the Civil War years, and the West, favoring the novels of Louis L'Amour.

His finest creation was a beautifully crafted plastic game that captivated both children and adults. He fashioned a series of plastic tracks of various widths that ran up, down and around in a series of loops. The player stood at one end and released a series of ball bearings of different sizes that traversed in an around the tracks, taking routes fitted to their size.

He built the game from clear plastic over a series of months. It measured nearly four feet in length, three feet high and two feet across and it sat on a platform so that players could feed the ball bearings while standing.

After he died, we donated the game to the Children's Museum in Indianapolis.

Bill took early retirement from Indiana Bell in 1975 after thirty-six years with the utility, mostly as an accountant. He was then fifty-nine and he explained that he had only about eight good hours a day and he saw no reason to waste it on a job he no longer enjoyed.

It was shortly before retirement that Bill again demonstrated his own method of dispensing justice.

Driving home from work one rush hour, he encountered the usual traffic slowdown where Pennsylvania Street narrows from three to two lanes just north of the bridge over Fall Creek. All of the motorists except one displayed patience waiting for their turn to merge with the traffic. The exception was a young man who kept inching in ahead of Bill, refusing to wait his turn. Bill tried to stop the driver by honking his horn and yelling at him. No luck. So Bill did the only thing Bill Connor would do: he hit the accelerator and crashed into the side of the man's car.

When he got home he called his insurance agent, Bob Dietz, and said:

"Bob, you'll be getting a claim on me. I hit a guy this afternoon, but forget it. This one's on me."

Retirement enabled Bill to improve his golf game. For years he had been trying to curb a vicious hook and the angry disposition that followed most rounds. Typical was an afternoon in the Riverside Golf Course clubhouse after one of those tense rounds. He bought one of the ham sandwiches prepackaged on the counter and noted that it contained a single slice of ham about the size of a silver dollar.

"Where's the ham?" Bill asked.

"You've got it," the counterman replied.

"Like hell I have," Bill snapped back. Then he swept all of the sandwiches on the floor and walked out.

Over the years Bill devised various experiments to straighten out his hook. He even had special oversized grips put on his clubs.

After he retired, he took a series of golf lessons from Tommy Vaughn, a golf professional and old friend from high school. It worked. With a new set of clubs, a new swing and a new attitude, he began shooting in the high seventies and low eighties, at least ten strokes better than he ever had in the past. With the hook behind him, he no longer was the angry golfer.

From then on playing golf with Bill became a pleasure, rather than an experience of undergoing three hours of tension.

In an ironic turnabout, Bill called me one morning a few weeks later to ask if I would like to join him for a game. I agreed and suggested that we ask Bob to join us. "Let's not," Bill replied. "You know how Bob loses his temper. He's not much fun to play with."

I had to stifle a laugh. Bob, the most easygoing of all the Connors, occasionally erupted on the golf course, but never was he as volatile as his brother.

Bill's good looks and generally pleasant personality made him attractive to women, but he shunned close relationships, preferring life as a bachelor. For many years he blamed Mother for his single state, contending that she objected to his dating Marty Bartlett, a beautiful and vivacious Butler coed, because she wasn't Catholic. But Mother contended that Marty's parents, and her grandmother in particular, objected because Bill was a Catholic. I think Marty was the only woman Bill ever seriously considered marrying. In time the romance cooled, but it was Bill's decision, not Mother's.

In time, we sensed that Bill used the excuse as a crutch against further entanglements. He never got serious with any other women, though he dated a few over the years. Maybe he sensed that his demanding personality would make him a difficult husband and father. While outwardly pleasant, Bill never seemed to be able to give of himself. He found it uncomfortable to embrace anyone; a trait common, to a lesser degree, with all of us with the possible exception of Nick.

Bill may have been the prototypical bachelor, but he developed a strong sense of family. He became the favorite uncle of his many nieces and nephews, spending hours at their football, basketball, kickball, volleyball and baseball games. He was especially close to Sally's children, who grew up three doors from the house he shared with Mother and Uncle Maurie on Evanston Avenue across from Broad Ripple Park.

He was generous with all of his nieces and nephews, making sure that each received a gift at Christmas. He supplied the money, his sisters and others did the shopping, wrapping and dispensing the gifts. Each niece and nephew received one hundred dollars at Christmas while enrolled in college and $500 when he or she graduated.

Bill remained close to Mother, though she exasperated him (as she had Dad) with her loose check writing and bookkeeping. She was a soft touch for any missionary group that sent a plea to help the Indians, blacks, homeless or orphans. Bill tried to establish some order in her charity.

Bill's life seemed never to be as rich and promising as it was when he was a student in college. He had been popular as an outstanding athlete and student leader in the all-boys Cathedral High School. But the lifelong shyness he showed around women was at work even then. Although class president in each of his four years there, Bill never found the nerve to ask a girl to either the junior prom or senior ball.

It was at Butler that life became rich and full for Bill. A three-year starter as center on the football team, though he carried only 145 pounds on his five-foot, nine-inch frame as a sophomore, he also became a campus leader and president of his fraternity, Phi Delta Theta.

Typical of Bill, though, was the lifelong resentment he felt about not being elected captain of the football team, an honor his brother Bob received the year after Bill graduated.

Life never was as satisfying for Bill as those halcyon days at Butler. Over the next forty years he recounted in detail events and activities of those college years, most of them centered on the football team. Nothing in life thereafter measured up to them.

One story he enjoyed telling concerned Jimmy McClure, who

grew up in our neighborhood and was a member of Bill's fraternity at Butler. At that time Jimmy had already won the world's table tennis championship. After Butler had played a basketball game against the University of Illinois one night, a group of Butler students showed up at the Phi Delt house on the Illinois campus. One of the local Phi Delts was loudly bragging about his prowess at ping pong and challenged any of the Butler visitors to a game. McClure accepted reluctantly and appeared to be an easy conquest for his opponent, purposely falling behind 20 to 0. Then McClure proceeded to win the next twenty-two points.

After graduation from Butler in 1939 Bill went to work for the telephone company, and Bob followed him there the following year. Trained as an accountant, Bill never particularly liked the work. He was drafted shortly after Pearl Harbor was bombed, and after being commissioned a lieutenant in the Army, he was sent to Harvard for a semester.

"I learned more there in one semester than I did in four years at Butler," he often remarked.

He spent the war years in an office building in New York City. When the war ended, he returned to work at the telephone company.

Perhaps his years in the Army provided enough traveling for Bill because he never expressed an interest in seeing much of the world beyond Indianapolis. He dismissed Europe because its cities were "dirty and ugly." He did visit some Civil War battlefields because of his interest in that war.

For a couple of years after retiring, Bill concentrated on putting together a photo history of the Connor family. He collected photos and snapshots from family members, and with earlier photos of parents and grandparents he filled ten large albums. Many of the photos carried appropriate and often humorous captions. One of the surprises in the collection was a full page of photos of Marty Bartlett, the beautiful coed he loved but gave up.

Either the nuns or Mother's dedication to the Catholic faith soured him on the Church for he rarely attended Mass. But as death approached, an old friend of the family, Father Kenny Sweeney, confided that Bill had met with him several times in that last year and that he had rejoined the Church.

The year before he died, Bill embarked on a project that turned out to be staggering considering his poor health. It was a courageous gesture. He spent months in the basement turning out individual Christmas toys and gifts for his brothers, sisters, in-laws, nieces, nephews, grand nieces and grand nephews—eighty-one in all. Each was painstakingly crafted of wood, sanded, stained and carefully finished.

Less than a month after that final Christmas he died. He was seventy-three.

At his funeral, his nephew, Bill Connor, then thirty-five, delivered a eulogy written by Tina Connor.

"We think Bill knew, either consciously or unconsciously, that this might be his last Christmas and he wanted each of us to have something from him that money couldn't buy. We're all so grateful for these gifts, especially after reading the journal (he kept a daily diary in his last years) and realizing how important this project was to him. He'd felt unwell and bone weary all year, but he really enjoyed creating these presents and he was determined to see the project to completion.

"Many families, even strong ones like ours, seem to drift apart after the matriarch or patriarch passes away. But this didn't happen in our family after Ag died—because we had Bill. He wasn't just any old bachelor uncle; he was the glue that held the joints, the common thread. He knew it, we think, and every time we glance to the shelf or the toy or the salt shaker he made, we'll remember him and the importance he placed on memory and family. And we'll stick together."

War Comes to Hampton Court

Life in Hampton Court was never the same after the Japanese bombed Pearl Harbor. Within a year most of the eligible young men left to join a branch of the service. It was four long years before they returned.

Nick and Bill were drafted into the Army in early 1942. I enlisted in the Army Air Corps in the summer of 1943. Sally joined the Waves in 1945.

Bob was never accepted for service because of a heart murmur. Being a young male civilian during the war years was painful for Bob, especially for such an outstanding athlete. He would come home depressed after someone asked why he wasn't in service, or after he had spent an evening with a friend home on leave.

The Connor males in Apartment 17 also left home to serve, Jack as a first lieutenant in the Air Force in El Paso, Gordon as a staff sergeant in the Air Force in India, Jim as an Aviation Radioman 3d Class, flying in a torpedo bomber, a TBF Avenger. Tom, the handsome all-American boy of the family, became a Navy pilot. As I have said, as a lieutenant junior grade, he flew off an aircraft carrier in the South Pacific one day and never returned. His plane was shot down over Okinawa. He was the only member of the two Connor families to die in the war. Tom was just twenty-three years old. His ship, the USS Yorktown, is now a memorial at the Charleston Naval Yards and his photo and name are engraved on the ship.

Nick was working at Centennial Press when he was drafted. Uncle Tommy wanted to apply for a deferment for him but Nick refused. He had no way of knowing that he would serve in the Army for more than four years, but when he learned he was going to be shipped overseas, he and Mary Harrison, his girl friend of more than three years, decided to get married secretly.

Their clandestine marriage at Camp Shelby, Mississippi on May 31, 1942, angered both of their parents, Mary's because Nick was a Catholic, and Mom because she resented not being told about it until after the marriage took place.

Mary recalled that she telephoned her adoptive parents, Orville and Hazel Myers, after the marriage and they were so distraught that she didn't expect either of them to meet her when she arrived home by train at Union Station. Orville was there, but Hazel "had taken to her bed in shock."

"Orville had some bad experience with Catholics early in life," Mary explained.

In time, though, they were reconciled. Hazel, in fact, confessed twenty-five years later when Nick died that she grieved more over his loss than she had when her husband Orville had died.

Mary recalled that she spent a trying two months on the East Coast over Thanksgiving and Christmas in 1942 when Nick was stationed at the Aberdeen Proving Grounds in Maryland before being shipped out to England. She never knew from one day to the next if she would see him again.

Only twenty-two years of age, she spent her days trying to find lodging while Nick was at the base. She walked up and down the streets of Havre de Grace knocking on doors in a house-to-house hunt for rooms. She finally succeeded when a woman named Hattie Crawford rented them a room.

Nick spent eighteen months in England as a captain and landed in France two months after D-Day. He spent a year and a half in Northern France, supplying the troops with ammunition. He wound up at an ordinance depot at Antwerp, Belgium, receiving and shipping ammunition to the Pacific after Germany surrendered. He came home with a Bronze Star.

Mary said she wondered if she would remember Nick's voice when he called after returning to the States in 1946 after three years in Europe. She did, of course.

Bill spent nearly all of his time in service behind a desk in Manhattan.

Sally served in the WAVES from April 1945 to June 1946. She

took her boot camp training at Hunter College in New York City, was trained as a medical corpsman at Bethesda Naval Hospital, and served as a corpsman at Great Lakes Naval Hospital.

"It was the first time I ever knew anything about lesbians," Sally said. "There were two girls in our bunkhouse who climbed in bed together," she recalled. "They didn't give us any trouble. They were pleasant enough."

Bill Lynch, who lived across the court from us and later married Sally, served in the Army in Europe as a civil engineer. And John Grande, who married Virginia after the war, spent thirteen months aboard a PT tender in the South Pacific as a repairman.

I enlisted in an Army reserve program the summer of 1943 two months before my eighteenth birthday and was sent to the University of Kentucky for a semester. That fall I went on active duty in the Army Air Corps, was trained as a high-speed radio operator and spent fourteen months at air bases in Natal and Recife, Brazil. My days were uneventful. I spent the morning taking routine weather reports in Morse Code, played basketball or tennis in the afternoon followed by a nap, and drank beer or watched a movie in the evening. Things got so boring that I read Rostand's *Cyrano de Bergerac* three times because it was the only book I could find on the base. For doing such meritorious work, I attained the rank of sergeant, though I never could understand why.

After the first year in Brazil it was difficult to hold on to the past. There were fewer letters to link me with home and friends. One day passed into another in boring routine. I had the feeling that I would be there forever because there was always the war in the Pacific that, we were told, would last for years. And I had neither the funds nor maturity to take advantage of travel throughout Brazil.

After Nick returned from Europe, he and Mary, like thousands of other returning veterans, found it nearly impossible to find a place to live because there had been almost no construction of new homes and apartments during the war. As a result, they lived for a time with us in Hampton Court.

The lack of privacy in a household with so many occupants was trying for them. Things hadn't improved much when Bob and Toni

Scheller were married on September 6, 1947, so they, too, lived with us for a few weeks before finding an apartment.

Toni said she suffered her first ulcer from living with all of us. Sally believed that it wasn't an ulcer that made Toni uncomfortable; it was being pregnant with her first child.

Nancy, that first child, was also the first of Mother's nineteen grandchildren. Bob and Toni had four more children: Bill, Tina, Bob and Kitzie. Nick and Mary had two boys, Nick and Steve. Sally and Bill had four children, Anne, Bill, Jeanie and Peggy. Virginia and John are the parents of two boys, Greg and Johnny.

In 1956 I married Patricia Alandt, a registered nurse who grew up in Irvington on the city's Eastside. We produced six little Connors: Carolyn, Julia Ann, Larry, Maureen, Janet and Michael.

Mother's nineteen grandchildren, in turn, produced forty-eight children of their own.

Sister Sally at Sweet 16

Bill (left) and Nick Connor as new lieutenants in the U.S. Army in early 1943.

(upper left) Mother and Uncle Bob Peelle in Hampton Court; (upper right) Virginia and Bo as Hampton Court teen-agers; (center) Nick and wife Mary during World War II; (above) All dressed up, the Connors gather in the Court in the late 1940s. (Rear) Bo, Bob, Nick and Bill; Sally (left) and Virginia flank Mother.

A serious Lawrence S. Connor in his 1943 graduation photo from Cathedral High School.

(left) Agnes Connor with her brothers, Maurie (left) and Bob Peelle, in 1940.

(center) One of the invitations to the annual Connor Christmas cocktail party in the 1950s.

(below) The six Connor siblings gather in Hampton Court in 1941: (from left) Bob, Virginia, Bo, Nick, Sally and Bill.

Forty-one Years At *The Star*

When we put out those three issues of the "Hampton Sentinel" and "The Court Reporter" in the summer of 1937 I must have gotten newspaper fever, or maybe I got it from watching *The Front Page* and *Foreign Correspondent* at the Cinema Theater. It all seemed so exciting and romantic.

I had been advised that the pay was poor but then Uncle Bob had convinced me that I should get into work that I would enjoy. So when I returned from three years in service, I enrolled at the University of Notre Dame, thanks to the GI Bill, to study journalism with the aim of getting a job on a newspaper, specifically one on *The Indianapolis Star*.

Growing up in Hampton Court in the thirties and forties helped to prepare me for the work. I had learned how to deal with authority at home and in service. The nuns and brothers and parents had stressed discipline and hard work. I looked at a career in journalism as something of a vocation, a way to serve.

I was fortunate and was hired as a cub reporter on *The Star* in the fall of 1949. Jobs were hard to get because papers had been rehiring reporters and copy editors who had been in service. I'm sure it helped that Mother had worked with the editor, James A. Stuart, in the years before she married.

It was a heady time. What did it matter that the pay was meager (forty-two dollars a week) or the work on nights and weekends? I was a newspaperman. And for the next forty-one years I would continue as a newspaperman in a series of jobs that were grueling, frustrating, maddening—but almost always interesting and sometimes even exciting.

If the news today was uneventful, there was always tomorrow. There were so many satisfactions: exposes that led to civic improvements, breaking major stories, being an insider on events, dealing with interesting and important people, working with even more interesting people. It was rich for the ego, too. There were the bylines, the comments about my stories. Even watching someone on a bus read a story that I had a hand in developing gave me a charge.

I didn't realize it at the time but *The Star* wasn't much of a paper when I joined it that fall, but then most medium-sized city papers were hardly distinguished. Two-section papers of twenty-four and twenty-eight pages were common. The papers were recovering from the war when reduced and inexperienced staffs were putting them out. *The Star* had spent the war years publishing mostly wire copy and limping along with a few decent reporters as stars and a support crew of aged and uninspired reporters and copy editors, many with drinking problems.

The paper was being run by a volatile Irishman, Robert P. Early, then in his third year as managing editor. Early had been with the paper since 1927. His brother Maurice wrote a daily Page One political column. A desk pounder, Early terrorized the staff with his profane outbursts for thirty-four years. Next to Bob Early my Dad looked like St. Francis.

Bob Early was typical of the editors of his time: stern, loud, demanding, unforgiving. The expression that "News is what the managing editor says it is" was certainly true at *The Star*.

The staff did what he and, to a lesser extent, the publisher, Eugene C. Pulliam, demanded. Early didn't encourage individual initiative. Don't get fancy; just get the facts, get them first, and tell them in clear, simple and accurate prose. Bylines were restricted to outstanding work and only one to an issue of the paper. That he ran the paper with absolute control was both his strength and his weakness. The paper improved under his direction because he drove the staff to cover the news thoroughly—and always to get it first. But Early failed to tap the brains and creativity in the staff. Still it took a strong hand to build the paper in those years. Early demanded results and he got them.

There were no real guidelines for hiring. Copy boys with high school educations became reporters and photographers, and some of them excelled. Not so with some of the "reformed" alcoholics that Early—in some of his more charitable moments—hired to give them one last chance. Most were gone after the first paycheck.

The reportorial staff in the City Room was mostly young and male; the Copy Desk mostly old and male. Aside from the five women who made up the Society Department, the paper had only five women reporters and copy editors and no blacks.

Businesses were sacred, especially businesses that advertised in the paper. *The Star* had its favorite persons and a few sacred cows and on rare occasions we would get the word to keep somebody's name (usually a Democrat) out of the paper. Education coverage was simple: a general assignment reporter who was free that night was assigned to cover the Indianapolis School Board meeting. Religion was restricted to the Saturday church page.

The paper was full of police news, stories about a two-headed baby at Petersburg, bizarre murders, car crashes and fires. We devoted a lot of space to local government and politics.

There was always some laudable crusade Bob Early dreamed up. Yard Parks ("the make your yard a park" campaign) seemed to go on forever. Under the leadership of a forceful woman, Mrs. B. Lynn Adams a civic leader, Yard Parks at one time had thirty-two divisions: Motor Truck, Industrial, Restaurant and Drive-in and whatever group could aid in the crusade to clean up the city. Few organizations escaped the hand of B. Lynn Adams. She arranged for distribution of flower seeds to kick off Yard Parks' annual campaign. There were contests for the cleanest drive-ins; thousands of boys and girls were enlisted to participate in spring cleanup efforts. The major goal each year was the coveted Clean City award from the National Clean-up, Paint-up, Fix-up Bureau. Stories recounting those efforts seemed endless. But the city won the prize.

The daylight running lights campaign got rolling in 1963. In nine months we carried ninety-two stories about the safety device, a little white light that fit into the center of the car's grill to alert oncoming drivers. Each day Early ordered stories to keep the drive alive, enlisting civic support wherever it could be coerced. Traffic safety officials fell in line, as did optometrists, politicians, service clubs, and truckers. We even induced 500-Mile champion Rodger Ward to get on board.

Because the stories were so uninspiring as news, the city editor assigned cub reporters to the daily task. When running lights were Early's crusade, I was the city editor. Enthusing some hapless reporter to chase down Early's latest target turned me into a second-rate diplomat.

Establishing The Ruins at Holliday Park was another of Early's projects; an endeavor that attracted Early's attention off and on for twenty years. It was directed by one of the city's celebrated artists, colorful, flamboyant Elmer Taflinger. He had a vision of relocating prized limestone statues taken from a razed building in New York City and displaying them in a "ruins" setting in Holliday Park.

Early was somewhat in awe of "Taf" and any complaint the artist had about such roadblocks as lack of cooperation from the park department brought an order from Early to "send somebody out there to get to the bottom of this."

The Ruins finally were completed in 1979. And the citizenry were expected to appreciate its charms for many years. Alas, the display fell into disrepair over the years and some Holliday Park lovers have suggested it be leveled and the statues relocated at the park entrance. Such talk borders on heresy.

Bob Early was big on solving murders, too. If the murder victim was someone of note and the police didn't come up quickly with an arrest, Early dispatched his police reporters to track down countless angles that he dreamed up.

The paper's efforts irritated the police department, but sometimes they paid off. In the 1950s the body of Dorothy Poore, an eighteen-year-old Clinton girl, was found stuffed in a drawer in a Claypool Hotel room. The case dominated the front page for weeks. The cops weren't having any luck finding the suspected killer, a man who had registered at the hotel as Jack O'Shea, so *Star* reporters quickly joined the search. One of them, Charles G. Griffo, deduced that O'Shea was an alias, and he discovered his real name by comparing O'Shea's handwriting with one at another hotel registered by a man named Victor Hale Lively. Lively was captured and convicted.

Bob Early also felt it necessary each time the Indiana General Assembly met that the legislators should pass a few bills that he believed would benefit the citizenry, if not *The Star*. It was up to the reporters assigned to cover the General Assembly to make certain that the legislators complied.

We had a one-man business staff who frequently assembled his column with handouts from local businesses. The Society Department concentrated on weddings and items about social affairs. The arts and cultural scene, such as it was, was handled by Corbin Patrick, who oversaw the city's cultural growth for more than sixty years as *The Star*'s drama critic. In the fifties, Pat had the help of two aides. The five or six-man sports staff devoted its attention to local high school sports, I. U., Purdue and Butler, and the 500-Mile Race.

For years photographers—"hypo sniffers"—were merely tolerated when they weren't being browbeaten by editors. In fact during and after World War II, the paper had only one full-time photographer, Joe Cravens. The photo staff had grown to four or five by the time I was hired, but it was years before the paper finally appreciated their value.

Some of the old *Front Page* atmosphere was still evident in those early years. The city room was crowded (and still is) and noisy. Editors yelled at reporters and copy boys. Teletype machines clicked out copy from the wire services, and reporters pounded out stories on Royal typewriters. Just about everyone smoked, so a haze hung over the desks at six o'clock when the staff was working on the bulldog edition. The linoleum-covered floors were littered with cigarette butts and scraps of copy paper that missed the trash cans.

We were always short on desks, so most of the young reporters shared them. My deskmate was Mary Jordan, the attractive church editor, who left a note in my typewriter one night: "Stay out of my drawers." I complied.

The Star had its share of colorful characters. On slow Sundays gravel-voiced Dick Roberts, then an assistant city editor, found ways to entertain the staff. When word was out that Muzak was being considered throughout the building, rewriteman Leon Russell, a fussy, middle-aged bachelor, became alarmed. Roberts and others led Leon to believe the music would be piped into the city room.

On the following Sunday Roberts rigged up a record player in the artist's shack. When Leon, whose musical tastes ran to Gilbert and Sullivan, loped down the hall on his way into the city room, the record player began bellowing out some early rock and roll. Russell became so incensed that he bashed his fist through one of the walls. It took a lot of reassurance that the city room would be music-free before Leon settled down.

The well-educated and articulate Roberts spent other slow nights composing bogus news stories to entertain the staff. When Bernie Wynn, a reporter, called in sick one night, Roberts turned to his Royal and typed:

If you could see little Bernie Wynn, you would cry.
He is pathetic.
Little Bernie has the affliction which afflicts so many pathetic little tykes.
Yet he is brave and doesn't complain.
Much.
He has the crud.
Thousands of moppets like Bernie have the crud.
If they have the crud, that is what makes them like him.
Give to crud.
Give until it hurts.
See the 30-hour Crudathon for crud victims, starting tonight
on television sponsored by The Indianapolis Star.

Roberts, a one-time liberal who now turns out serious conservative editorials, came up with this mock *Readers Digest* table of contents on a night when the news was slow:

It's Fun to be Wretched
Enjoy Your Cancer
The Most Unforgettable Incident I Ever Forgot
The Woodchuck—Mother Nature's Fraud
TVA—Socialized Kilowatts
What Became of Judge Crater?
Psychoanalysis and Suckers
I Lost One Billion Dollars
Poverty Means Happiness
Hitler's Last Thrill
Is Russia Rushin?
Funerals Can Be Gay
Why Not a Hadacol Bomb?

We had a wonderful city editor. His name was Lowell Parker. He acted as a buffer between Early and the staff. He knew when to comply with Early's memos, and when to file them in his reject drawer. Parker had been an ace rewriteman before he joined the Coast Guard during the war. He didn't take journalism too seriously; he carried out Early's directives, though he knew how to marshal the staff on major stories. Good looking and gregarious, Parker loved a party and he was a surprisingly adept ballroom dancer. When a report came over the wire that the wild and wicked movie actor Errol Flynn had died, Parker shook his head sadly and remarked, "There aren't many of us left."

Most of our journalistic efforts were aimed at scooping the opposition; in those days it was the self-described liberal *Indianapolis Times*, and *The Star's* sister paper, *The Indianapolis News*, which Pulliam had purchased in 1948. Television was just getting started and radio news was mostly a rehash of what had been in the papers.

We couldn't get enough of the business. Scooping *The Times*, making Page One with a story, or turning out a feature that brought a compliment from Parker only made us want more, so we'd be out the next day chasing down news.

The staff was big on parties. Because many of the reporters worked until eleven o'clock, it was not unusual for the gatherings to go on until three in the morning. We battled *The Times* staff on the job but partied with them on the weekends. Few *News* staffers attended. In those years *News* staffers came across as superior and had little taste for mingling with the rest of us.

Or, after work we would gather in one of the dingy taverns in the neighborhood and rehash the day's efforts. We listened to older staffers recount colorful stories which got embellished with each telling. Vladimir Posvar, whose varied career included stints on several newspapers and an extended stay in the military, was a copy editor on *The Star* at that time. He had a score of tales. He recalled that a co-worker on the *New York Mirror* got a ten dollar bonus from the publisher, William Randolph Hearst, for a headline —"Baby Gives Bride Away"—that took up the entire front page of the tabloid. The story inside recounted that the pregnant bride was trussed so tightly that she went into labor on the altar.

"Pos" never lost his military bearing, often greeting persons by throwing back his shoulders and clicking his heels. He once dressed down one of the paper's security guards for not being in proper uniform. Once "Pos" was fired from a Cleveland paper after greeting Eleanor Roosevelt's arrival in the city with an editorial calling for a twenty-one gun salute that went on "boom, boom" twenty-one times. Because Mrs. Roosevelt told someone she liked it, he retained his job.

It was all great fun but too many reporters and editors later paid heavily for reliance on the bottle in broken marriages and lost jobs.

Like most cub reporters at *The Star*, I spent the first year working the night police beat, racing around the city from six o'clock until two in the morning covering murders, holdups, traffic accidents and fires. I next was assigned to cover the mayor and the various boards in City Hall. I had to be doubly accurate when covering a park or zoning board meeting because Mother was serving on those boards. True to form, she seemed to be most interested in the poor and dispossessed who came before the boards.

By 1953 I was brought into the office to serve as an assistant city editor. My reporting career at *The Star* was over, though I did report as a stringer for the *National Observer* in its fifteen years of existence and retold some local crimes for detective magazines, jobs I took on to help support a wife and six children. I remained in different editing positions for the next thirty-seven years.

The paper was more relaxed in those early years. I was allowed, even encouraged, to take a three-month leave in the spring of 1952 to tour Europe.

Though I never saw him in the newsroom in all the years I worked there, Eugene C. Pulliam's presence was always with us. He was an interesting figure. Born in a dugout in Kansas, he was the son of a Methodist minister and part of his zeal may have been traced to his early years. He was one of the last of the publishers in the image of Hearst and Pulitzer and *The Chicago Tribune's* Colonel McCormick, outspoken publishers who used their newspapers as organs for their views.

In the sixty-three years that he spent publishing newspapers,

Pulliam at one time or another owned forty-six newspapers along with some radio stations. He bought *The Star* and two Muncie papers in 1944, two papers in Phoenix in 1946, and *The News* in 1948. Buying the Phoenix papers was "like marrying a Rockefeller," he often remarked.

The crewcut Pulliam dominated any gathering with his strong physical presence and his outspoken manner. He was paternalistic with both his employees (it was always "the *Star-News* family") and his subscribers. He regularly enlightened his readers with lucid Page One editorials. On an October Sunday in 1971 he used the entire front page for an editorial he wrote headlined: "Will The Federal Bureaucracy Destroy Individual Freedom In America?" It carried an editor's note: "This full page editorial is unique in newspaper publishing." There was no question about that. Pulliam was then eighty-two years old, but he still had the fire. And the question he asked still remains an open one.

For years *The Star's* front page was dominated by a three-column editorial cartoon lampooning liberals drawn by the paper's long-time cartoonist, Charlie Werner.

Terse memos from ECP would come to the City Desk through Early's office, this one in October 1970:

"Get shot of Senator Hartke with Coretta Scott King. Arrange for a reporter to be along to ask Hartke, 'Just how do you stand on busing, Senator Hartke?' Make certain the question is asked in the presence of Mrs. King."

Senator Hartke was a frequent target of Pulliam's memos. And so were the Kennedys.

The Star took a lot of well-deserved criticism for its coverage of the Indiana primary in 1968 because the paper was so blatantly anti-Robert Kennedy in its news coverage. At one stop Kennedy told a group of local ministers that *The Star* and *The News* were "the worst newspapers in the country."

I was sometimes asked, usually by Democrats, how I could work for "that Republican rag." I brushed them off by telling them that it was better to be working on the inside than sitting outside and carping about the paper. While the paper's use of its news columns to carry out the publisher's causes sometimes damaged the paper's credibility, *The Star's* reportorial staff was winning national awards for its work, as well as most of the state's journalism awards.

Early's hard-driving demands paid off in 1964 when *The Star* won the National Headliners Award for its coverage of the explosion at the Fairgrounds Coliseum on Halloween night, October 31, 1963. A butane explosion that erupted during the finale of a *Holiday on Ice* show took the lives of seventy-four spectators and injured nearly four hundred. In less than two hours the staff—many called out of their beds by Early—raced to the Coliseum, to the hospitals and into the newsroom and turned out a complete account of the disaster, including photos and a list of many of the dead and injured.

In 1974 the paper won the Pulitzer Prize for its expose of corruption in the Indianapolis Police Department. A five-person team spent months investigating the widespread abuses.

Little by little *The Star* was becoming an outstanding newspaper.

Pulliam was generous and kind to his employees. Few were ever fired. Pay scales increased annually; generous pension and health plans were provided and well-equipped recreation areas for employees and their families were opened both in Indianapolis and in Phoenix. He established scholarships for carriers and children of employees and set up the Pulliam Fellowship program for young journalists just graduating from college.

But the paper's rigid editorial opposition to aid from the Federal government, while the rest of the country was grabbing all it could, tended to hold back the city's progress.

The tenor of the paper changed after the death of Pulliam at the age of eighty-six in 1975. His son, Eugene S. Pulliam, who had been associate publisher, succeeded him. He was much different from his father; quiet and moderate, he didn't play the role of political kingmaker. Although his political views were conservative, he kept them confined to the editorial pages. Treating the paper as something of a public trust, he gave his editors the freedom to turn *The Star* into a first-rate newspaper. As a result, the paper's credibility was enhanced.

The paper had evolved over the last few years of Gene Sr.'s life.

The staff was greatly expanded to cover a city that was growing in every direction. We had gone electronic a few years earlier. Typewriters and teletype machines were gone, replaced by computers. Some of the noise was gone but the telephones continued their constant ringing. There was carpeting on the floors and the place even became smoke-free.

In 1979 the editor, Frank Crane, retired and I moved into his office after sixteen grueling years as city editor.

I loved being editor, overseeing the editorial pages, writing editorials and a column when the notion hit me. They gave me a new chair (I think it cost $400), new drapes in the office and the freedom to tell Washington how to run the country every day. The telephone rarely rang.

Too good to last. Three months after I moved into Frank's office, Bob Early decided suddenly to retire after fifty-two years at *The Star*. He was seventy-four and still as strong willed as ever. I got his job and a chance to make further changes that I and the staff felt were needed.

We completely rebuilt the photography department, and hired more reporters and editors, many of them women and blacks, though the business office thought the editorial department wildly extravagant.

The paper was spending money on new electronic equipment throughout the building and getting ready to spend millions on new offset presses.

Most of the changes were also being made in major papers all over the country. They were hiring graphics editors, artists and newspaper designers, a reaction to television. Newspapers no longer were always first with the news; they had to provide more stories about why things were happening. The electronic tools allowed papers to quickly devise graphs and charts to illustrate complex issues, most of them in color.

There was some anxiety about changing the front page. It had always been dominated by two eight-column headlines; one in bold ninety-six-point type, the other in seventy-two point italic. Very often the news simply didn't warrant large headlines. Some Mondays readers were faced with headlines proclaiming, "Two Die In Indochina" or "Typhoon Hits Martinique," stories that never got a call the rest of the week. Dropping the "flags" gave us more latitude in making up the front page.

The Star team that produced the long-running series on police corruption was instrumental in founding Investigative Reporters and Editors (IRE) in 1976. Myrta Pulliam, the third generation of Pulliams on the paper, and reporter Harley Bierce, were two of the four IRE founders. Myrta served as its president. IRE now has 4,000 members.

Many of the changes at *The Star* were made to keep up with what was happening in Indianapolis. The city was in a boom period. Construction downtown and in the suburbs was exploding. The arts were flourishing with new museums, new theaters, opera, ballet, and dance groups. The city attracted professional sports and was luring amateur sports organizations to locate in the city. It took a staff of twenty-five to keep up with all of the sporting events. The Women's Department got males on its staff and became the Lifestyle Department. Readers demanded more business news, so a separate business department with a nine-person staff was formed.

Soon the city did indeed become the scene of major sporting events, including the National Sports Festival in 1982 and the prestigious Pan-American Games in 1987.

The Star outdid itself in the coverage of these important events, turning out special sections throughout the sixteen days of the Pan-Am Games, including a daily wrapup of events written in Spanish for athletes, officials and fans from Latin American countries.

The paper earned its second Pulitzer Prize for a series of stories in 1990 about medical malpractice in the state.

That same year I kept the promise I had made to myself years earlier and retired on my sixty-fifth birthday.

For a long time my wife insisted that *The Star* came first with me; the family second. I, of course, always disagreed but looking back on those forty-one years I'd have to admit that in a real sense *The Star* ruled my life. But what a great life it was.

- 30 -

It is 1995 now and the family of six that grew up in Hampton Court a half century ago is down to three: Sally, Virginia and me. Nick died on August 8, 1967 at the age of fifty-four. Bob was sixty-four when he died in 1982, and Bill died in 1989. He was seventy-three.

The three of us who remain shall soon know if those promises of eternal life, first made by Mother and the priests and sisters at 14th and Meridian streets, will be realized.

I'm hard at work as City Editor in the 1960s.

Ace reporter Carolyn Pickering Lautner and I gingerly attempt a two-step in 1971.

Light heavyweight boxer Willie Besmanoff gets expert advice on his upcoming bout with champion Archie Moore in Indianapolis in 1960. The advice from Connor and sports editor Bob Collins was ineffective. Willie lost on a TKO in the 10th Round.

A young Bob Collins, longtime sports editor of *The Star*, takes a minute to converse with me about some high-level matter at the City Desk.

George Bush visits *The Star* while campaigning for the Republican nomination for President in 1980. He lost his bid to Ronald Reagan.

I get a firm handshake from Governor Robert Orr in his Statehouse office.

(left) The eccentric, brilliant, fun-loving Richard R. Roberts has been a fixture at *The Star* for decades.

(center) After announcing his retirement as managing editor of *The Star* in 1979 after 34 years in the job, Bob Early poses with his successor (left) and my successor as editor, John H. Lyst.

(below) *The Star's* City Room staff assembles for a group photo in 1979.

Agnes Peelle Connor — as we remember her.